DELINQUENT CRIMINAL DEBT: WHAT'S OWED? WHAT'S PAID?

TUESDAY, JUNE 28, 1994

U.S. SENATE,
COMMITTEE ON GOVERNMENTAL AFFAIRS,
Washington, DC.

The Committee met, pursuant to notice, at 10:19 a.m., in room SD–342, Dirksen Senate Office Building, Hon. Byron Dorgan presiding.

Present: Senators Dorgan, Glenn, and Cohen.

Senator DORGAN. I would like to begin this hearing on behalf of the Governmental Affairs Committee and Chairman Glenn. Other members of the Committee will join us. We have a vote in progress in the Senate and just cast the vote and other members will be here shortly.

OPENING STATEMENT OF SENATOR DORGAN

Senator DORGAN. This morning the Governmental Affairs Committee will examine why uncollected Federal criminal debt has risen to nearly $4 billion. We are only collecting between 1 and 5 cents on the dollar from people convicted of Federal crimes who are both fined and ordered to make restitution payments.

The Committee will also examine why the Government has failed to establish a national computer network to better track and collect Federal court fined and restitution orders. Finally the Committee will review the potential impact of current seize and forfeiture statutes on criminal debt collection and the negative impact on the Crime Victims Fund when outstanding Federal debt goes uncollected. I am concerned that the Department of Justice and the Administrative Office of the U.S. Court does not have adequate systems in place to ensure that Federal criminal debt, both fines and restitution, are more aggressively tracked and paid.

Beginning in 1986, the staff of the AOUSC painted a picture of an archaic, decentralized nonsystem which let many offenders escape paying what they owe their victims and the Federal Government. They were right back in 1986, but 8 years later, despite access to $19 million in startup funds, we still have an archaic, decentralized nonsystem which allows many criminal offenders to escape paying what they owe their victims and the Federal Government.

Today we will hear testimony from the GAO, the Government Accounting Office. They will present an update of their earlier report of August 1993 on the National Fine Center entitled "Expectations High, but Development Behind Schedule." Mr. Henry Wray,

Director of the GAO's Administration of Justice Issues Office will testify that outstanding criminal debt grew from $300 million in 1985 to $3.6 billion in 1993. While it may be extremely difficult to assess how effectively Federal agencies collect criminal debts or how much of the outstanding debt is realistically collectible, the GAO believes the Government systems for imposing, collecting, enforcing and accounting for criminal debt deserves greater scrutiny.

The GAO will further testify that the most important step in enhancing debt collection is to make the National Fine Center fully operational. The USAOC now is developing a new two-part implementation plan and expects that the first phase of the National Fine Center will be operational by September 1, 1996, nearly 2 years from now; almost 9 years after legislation was creating the National Fine Center enacted by the Congress. Ironically, the first phase of this two-part implementation plan will not be automated.

It is important to note that the Administrative Office of the Courts have missed every timetable and milestone for the establishment of the National Fine Center. In fact, the Administrative Office has recently decided to abandon its $6 million pilot project and begin the entire process from scratch, I understand.

Forfeiture authorities are an important tool used by law enforcement to deprive criminals of the proceeds in the instruments of their crimes. Under forfeiture statutes assets can be seized before or even without a criminal conviction, thereby preventing diversion of a defendant's assets prior to conviction. Most forfeiture proceeds are used to fund law enforcement activities and do not count against an agency's appropriation.

In 1992, the GAO testified that the perpetrators of the Nation's savings and loan fiasco and other instances of financial fraud paid only about 4 cents on every dollar in fines, restitution and other payments they owed the American taxpayers. Recent statistics collected by our Federal law enforcement officials suggest that the Federal Government's dismal record in this area remains unchanged. The aggregate fines and restitution orders imposed on major financial institution fraud cases between October 1988 and today is about $1.9 billion and we've collected a mere $49.3 million or less than 3 percent of the total.

The GAO will testify that of the top 50 pending criminal debts owed to the Federal Government, fines and restitution orders, less than 1 percent has been collected. Of the top 50 criminal debts, 36 involve financial institution fraud cases with $608 million ordered and $4 billion collected or 0.6 of 1 percent collected.

I think I would like if I could have someone go down and show some charts, I would like to review some of this with some charts that would make it more easily understandable and raise some of the questions that we will be discussing today. I wonder if we could have this set of charts put up.

The first chart shows the 50 largest criminal debts owed to the United States, and this is from the GAO analysis of the Justice Department. The 50 largest criminal debts owed to the U.S., $822 million ordered and $4.1 million collected as of May 31, 1994. That's one-half of 1 percent that has been collected.

Of those 50 largest criminal debts, 36 of them involve financial institution fraud debts. So if you take at look at the 50 largest

S. Hrg. 103–1046

DELINQUENT CRIMINAL DEBT: WHAT'S OWED? WHAT'S PAID?

HEARING

BEFORE THE

COMMITTEE ON GOVERNMENTAL AFFAIRS UNITED STATES SENATE

ONE HUNDRED THIRD CONGRESS

SECOND SESSION

TUESDAY, JUNE 28, 1994

Printed for the use of the Committee on Governmental Affairs

U.S. GOVERNMENT PRINTING OFFICE

80–935 CC WASHINGTON : 1995

For sale by the U.S. Government Printing Office
Superintendent of Documents, Congressional Sales Office, Washington, DC 20402
ISBN 0-16-047390-X

80-935 - 95 - 1

COMMITTEE ON GOVERNMENTAL AFFAIRS

JOHN GLENN, Ohio, *Chairman*

SAM NUNN, Georgia
CARL LEVIN, Michigan
JIM SASSER, Tennessee
DAVID PRYOR, Arkansas
JOSEPH I. LIEBERMAN, Connecticut
DANIEL K. AKAKA, Hawaii
BYRON L. DORGAN, North Dakota

WILLIAM V. ROTH, Jr., Delaware
TED STEVENS, Alaska
WILLIAM S. COHEN, Maine
THAD COCHRAN, Mississippi
JOHN McCAIN, Arizona
ROBERT F. BENNETT, Utah

Leonard Weiss, *Staff Director*
Jeremy Bates, *Legislative Assistant*
Franklin G. Polk, *Minority Staff Director and Chief Counsel*
Michal Sue Prosser, *Chief Clerk*

CONTENTS

	Page
Opening statements:	
Senator Dorgan	1
Senator Glenn	5
Prepared statements:	
Senator Dorgan	3
Senator Cohen	19

WITNESSES

June 28, 1994

Henry R. Wray, Director, Administration of Justice Issues, U.S. General Accounting Office, accompanied by Steven C. Martin, Senior Evaluator, General Government Division; and Jan B. Montgomery, Assistant General Counsel, Office of General Counsel	7
Richard A. Ames, Assistant Director for Finance and Budget, U.S. Administrative Office of the Courts, accompanied by Peter G. McCabe, Assistant Director for Judges Programs and Nancy C. Fleetwood, Chief, Accounting and Financial Systems Division	16
Gerald M. Stern, Special Counsel, Financial Institution Fraud, Department of Justice, accompanied by Richard W. Sponseller, Deputy Director, Executive Office for U.S. Attorneys	20
David Beatty, Director of Public Affairs, National Victim Center	32

Alphabetical List of Witnesses

Ames, Richard A.:	
Testimony	16
Prepared statement	49
Beatty, David:	
Testimony	33
Prepared statement	70
Stern, Gerald M.:	
Testimony	20
Prepared statement	65
Wray, Henry R.:	
Testimony	7
Prepared statement	39

APPENDIX

Prepared statements of witnesses in order of appearance	39
Letter to Senator Dorgan, dated June 28, 1994, from Hon. Harris Wofford, Senator from the State of Pennsylvania	49
Letter with enclosures, dated June 13, 1994, to Senator McCain from L. Ralph Mecham, Director, Administrative Office of the United States Courts	53

debts, 36 of them involve financial institution fraud debts. The total there is $608 million ordered paid; $4 million collected or .6 of 1 percent.

Even if one excludes the largest financial institution fraud cases where the perpetrator is incarcerated, and that is the case in many cases, for those who are not incarcerated, $224 million has been ordered. Now these are people who are not now incarcerated. And 1.3 percent or $2.9 million have been collected.

The next chart reflects data collected by the Justice Department that totals all of the fines and the restitution orders imposed in all major savings and loans and bank fraud cases, all financial institution fraud cases, which I might say incidentally makes up a large part of the growth of Federal fines and restitution orders between October 1988 and May 1994. That is $1.96 billion. That is national restitution and fines that have been assessed on S&L and financial institution fraud cases; $1.96 billion ordered; $49.3 million collected or 2.5 percent has been collected on that which has been ordered.

The point of this hearing is to raise some questions about these issues and to try to determine where are we with respect to the National Fine Center. It is probably true that fines and restitutions ordered against people who are thrown in jail and have no assets will never be collected under any circumstances. I fully understand that and I accept that.

However, we've gone through a period of extraordinary greed in which we saw massive amounts of fraud. Two-thirds of the S&Ls that have failed in this country have some fraud involved. We have seen substantial fines levied against those who have bilked the American taxpayers, billions of dollars. And what we see in many cases is a very dismal collection rate, often less than a penny on a dollar is being collected. Is that all that can be collected? None of us have the foggiest idea. It seems like an unusually low rate. But we do not have any idea because we do not have a system that works.

I cannot today nor can Senator Glenn or others say, can we find in this system what is the age of these debts, the location, the address of the people who owe them? The fact is, the system is in disarray. Decentralized, it is still at the quill pen stage, and it desperately needs to change. And that was the purpose of the National Fine Center, $5 million of which has been spent out of funds that otherwise would go to the victims funds and we do not yet have a National Fine Center.

The purpose of this hearing is to raise a series of questions about that and understand where we are and where we are headed and how soon we will get there. That is opening for this hearing and now let me call on the Chairman of the Full Committee, Senator Glenn.

PREPARED STATEMENT OF SENATOR DORGAN

This morning the Governmental Affairs Committee will examine why the uncollected Federal criminal debt has risen to almost $4 billion. We are only collecting between one and five cents on the dollar from people convicted of Federal crimes.

The Committee will also examine why the Government has failed to establish a National Computer Network to better track and collect Federal court fine and restitution orders.

Finally, the Committee will review the potential impact of current seized and forfeiture statutes on criminal debt collection and, the negative impact on the Crime Victims Fund when outstanding Federal debt goes uncollected.

I am concerned that the Department of Justice (DOJ), and the Administrative Office of the United States Courts (AOUSC), does not have an adequate system in place to ensure that Federal criminal debt (fines and restitution), is more aggressively tracked and paid.

Beginning in 1986 the staff of the AOUSC painted a picture of an archaic, decentralized, non-system which let many offenders escape paying what they owe their victims and the Federal Government.

They were right back in 1986. But eight years later—despite access to $19 million in start-up funds, we still have an archaic, decentralized, non-system which allows many criminal offenders to escape paying what they owe their victims and the Federal Government.

Outstanding Debt

Today we will hear testimony from the General Accounting Office (GAO). They will present an update to their earlier report (Aug. 93), on the National Fine Center (NFC) entitled "Expectations High, but Development Behind Schedule".

Mr. Henry Wray, the Director of the GAO's Administration of Justice Issues Office, will testify that outstanding criminal debt grew from $0.3 billion in 1985 to $3.6 billion in 1993. While it may be extremely difficult to assess how effectively Federal agencies collect criminal debts or how much of the outstanding debt is realistically collectible, the GAO believes that the Government's systems for imposing, collecting, enforcing, and accounting for criminal debt deserves greater scrutiny.

National Fine Center

The GAO will further testify that the most important step in enhancing debt collection efforts is to make the NFC fully operational. The USAOC now is developing a new two-part implementation plan, and expects that the first phase of the NFC will be operational nationwide by September 1, 1996, almost nine years after legislation creating the NFC was enacted. Ironically, the first phase of this two-part implementation plan will not be automated.

It is important to note that the AOUSC has missed every timetable and milestone for the establishment of the NFC. In fact the AOUSC has recently decided to abandon its six million dollar pilot project and begin the entire process from scratch.

Asset Forfeiture Authorities

Forfeiture authorities are an important tool used by law enforcement to deprive criminals of the proceeds and instruments of their crimes. Under forfeiture statutes, assets can be seized before or even without a criminal conviction thereby preventing diversion of a defendant's assets prior to conviction. Most forfeiture proceeds are used to fund law enforcement activities and do not count against an agency's appropriation.

Financial Institution Fraud

In 1992, the GAO testified that the perpetrators of the Nation's savings and loan fiasco and other financial institution fraud had paid only about four cents on every dollar of fines, restitution and other payments they owed the American taxpayers.

Recent statistics collected by our Federal law enforcement officials suggest that the Federal Government's dismal record in this area remains unchanged. The aggregate fines and restitution orders imposed in major financial institution fraud cases between Oct. 1988 and today is about $1.96 billion, and we've only collected a mere $49.3 million or less than 3% of the total.

The GAO will testify that of the top 50 pending criminal debts (i.e. fines and restitution orders) owed to the Federal Government, less than 1 percent has been collected.

Of the top 50 criminal debts, 36 involve financial institution fraud cases, with $608 million ordered, and $4 million collected—a dismal .6 percent collection rate. Even if one discards the cases where the perpetrators are incarcerated, the Federal Government's collection of the debts is only 1.3 percent.

Restitution orders payable to the FDIC of $1 million or more for bank fraud: total nearly $400 million and only $19 million or 4.8 percent has been collected.

Restitution orders payable to the RTC of $1 million or more for thrift fraud total $385 million and, only $6 million or 1.5 percent, has been collected.

There are questions regarding the Federal Government's commitment to pursue collection. For example, it was reported that of the 200 U.S. Attorney's office prosecutors in south Florida, only 4 were assigned to pursue collections (the Miami Herald—Dec., 1993).

The Department's system of complying data on collection efforts is archaic. The Department continues to compile data on financial institution fraud cases through a system of "manual reporting " by the U.S. Attorney's office.

It's time to bring the Federal Government's debt collection tracking system into the 20th century. If there is one thing that the taxpayers of this country have a right to expect, it is that those who committed fraud in the savings and loan industry get the punishment that they deserve, and that we recover assets and ill-gotten gains held by such perpetrators.

OPENING STATEMENT OF CHAIRMAN GLENN

Chairman GLENN. Thank you very much, Senator Dorgan. Senator Dorgan is chairing the hearing this morning, but I wanted to stop by and give my support to what he is doing and make a couple of comments. I am sorry we were not here at the appointed hour, but there was a vote on the floor at 10 o'clock which was put off until 10:10 and then we voted and got here as soon as we could.

The Governmental Affairs Committee is charged with looking into efficiencies in Government. That is one of our mandates. Many people may figure that phase is an oxymoron in itself, efficiencies in Government. But this Committee has taken those words very seriously through the years and we have fought to make the Federal Government work better.

I know it is enticing for the press to concentrate on $90 screwdrivers and $7,000 coffee pots and other excesses that come out occasionally, but we have worked to rid the Government of instances of waste, fraud, and abuse that have become all too familiar as part of our Government system. Rather than concentrating on specific items, we have tried to make a better system through the new procurement legislation which is working its way through the Government now.

That legislation passed in the House yesterday. It passed here in the Senate about a month or so ago. We passed the Chief Financial Officer's Act several years ago which Charles Bowsher, head of the General Accounting Office, said was the best step forward in financial management in the Federal Government in the last 40 years. We passed the IG Act and so on. I will not go into a litany of all the things we have done here, but they are what we call sometimes the "grunt work" of Government. We try to set up the systems to do the kind of work that will let us operate more efficiently in the future.

Today though, the Committee will be focusing on Government waste. And once again it is not front page, and probably will not make any big headlines, but it really is a lack of efficiency by the Government. Put differently, it is a loss of opportunity for the Government to recover well over $3 billion that belongs to the American people.

Every year Federal judges impose substantial fines on persons who have been convicted of illegal activity. The prosecutors for whom fine collection is not a priority or who simply may be overworked, seem to not pursue collection of these fines in any meaningful way. The Department of Justice acknowledges that it has recovered less than 1 percent of the $608 million due to the Government from the top 50 criminal fraud cases. That is less than 1 percent, less than 1 percent recovered.

As a result, the Government is being deprived of millions, maybe even billions of dollars which could be used to fund the many important programs which serve the people of this country and for which we lack sufficient funding. This return of ill-gotten gains must be part of the punishment followup. Otherwise, you set up a system that says "serve your time, but then retire on the loot." And the "loot" should be coming back to the Government in all of these cases.

We thought that in 1987, upon the establishment of the National Fine Center, that the Government's collection rate would greatly improve. That was the purpose of the Fine Center. I am disappointed this has not been the case. I am told that after 7 years and some $5 million, the National Fine Center has scrapped most of its work and is now starting again from ground zero without ever having implemented a single overall program. Why? I think we need to know the answers to that and perhaps we will find out this morning.

I understand that coordinating and standardizing procedures from 94 U.S. attorney offices across this country is a daunting task. But I cannot understand why it should have taken 7 years and $5 million to produce little, if any, result.

I am also glad we will be addressing the issue of extremely high fines and orders of restitution that cannot be paid by defendants, even at the time they are imposed. There is clearly a tension between requiring a criminal to pay what is owed and being realistic about what debt we carry on our books as collectible. We want to be realistic in what we expect without letting anyone off the hook.

I want to commend Senator Dorgan for his hard work in this area of debt collection. He was a leader in the House in looking into these areas of fat, fraud, waste and abuse in Government. He came over to the Senate and we talked not long after he was sworn in, about what work he might undertake here in the Senate. He has been hard at it ever since he got here and is doing an excellent job. So I want to commend him for his work.

I believe the statutory framework already exists to do an effective job of fine collection . For our witnesses this morning, I would be happy to consider any legislative proposals which the witnesses may submit that may improve our activity in this area. I support you in what I know is a difficult job and looking forward to the time that we will be convening such hearings to discuss the success of the Government in collecting outstanding criminal debt.

So at this hearing, we need answers to what is realistic in criminal debt collection? What is doable? And then let us do it or stop pretending we are doing something constructive when we are not. So those are some of the things that we want to look into this morning.

I have some other commitments this morning. I will try and stop back later, but Senator Dorgan, I want to commend you for the outstanding job you are doing in looking into some of these areas. Thank you.

Senator DORGAN. Senator Glenn, thank you very much. Our first panel will be the Government Accounting Office, Mr. Henry Wray, the Director of the Administration of Justice Issues of the GAO; Mr. Steven Martin, who is accompanying Mr. Wray; and Ms. Jan Montgomery, both of whom are with the GAO. Senior Evaluator, Mr. Martin is with the General Government Division; and Assistant General Counsel of the Office of General Counsel is Ms. Montgomery.

Mr. Wray, welcome and your entire statement will be made a part of the permanent record. You may summarize, as you wish.

TESTIMONY OF HENRY R. WRAY,[1] DIRECTOR, ADMINISTRATION OF JUSTICE ISSUES, GENERAL GOVERNMENT DIVISION, U.S. GENERAL ACCOUNTING OFFICE, ACCOMPANIED BY STEVEN C. MARTIN, SENIOR EVALUATOR, GENERAL GOVERNMENT DIVISION, U.S. GENERAL ACCOUNTING OFFICE, AND JAN B. MONTGOMERY, ASSISTANT GENERAL COUNSEL, OFFICE OF GENERAL COUNSEL, U.S. GENERAL ACCOUNTING OFFICE

Mr. WRAY. Thank you, Senator Dorgan. We are pleased to appear before you today to discuss the Federal Government's criminal debt collection efforts. Our debt collection consists primarily of fines and restitution orders. Criminal fines are payable to the Federal Government and most fine payments are deposited into the Fine Victims Fund which in turn is used primarily for grants to provide compensation and assistance to victims involved in crime. The Crime Victims Fund also supports Judicial Branch that collects activities which I will touch on shortly.

Restitution is payable directly or indirectly to parties who suffered financial loss as a result of the crime for which the defendant was convicted and restitution is designed to compensate them for that loss. In deciding whether to impose fines and restitution and then arriving at the amounts, the sentencing judge is required to take into account a number of factors, including the nature of the offense, the losses suffered and the defendant's present and future ability to pay.

The judge considers recommendations from the U.S. Attorney and information contained in the presentence report prepared by the probation office in reaching sentencing decision. The presentence report includes information on the defendant's financial condition. Fines and restitutions generally are due immediately upon imposition of sentence, unless the court provides for payment at a specific future date or in installments.

U.S. Attorney is responsible for taking enforcement action on delinquent criminal debt. However, responsibility for initially receiving and processing criminal debt payments is fragmented. Depending on the particular arrangements in each of the 94 Federal judicial districts, the local offices of one of three different agencies—the U.S. Attorney's office, the probation office, or the clerk of court—may be responsible for receiving and accounting for fine payments.

Senator DORGAN. Who makes that decision?

Mr. WRAY. The agencies work it out themselves right now on a district by district basis by memorandum of agreement. Also, de-

[1] The prepared statement of Mr. Wray appears on page 39.

pending on how the sentencing order is written, criminal debtors may make restitution payments through one of these three agencies, again depending on the agreement in effect, or they may make payment directly to the victim.

The Criminal Fine Improvement Act of 1987 was defined to centralized responsibility for initial criminal debt collection in the Administrative Office of the U.S. Courts. Congress contemplated that the Administrative Office would establish a single national center within the judicial branch for processing fines, restitution and other criminal debt. As you have mentioned earlier, Senator Dorgan, the Administrative Office is developing the National Fine Center to achieve this objective. The Fine Center is to track and collect criminal debts for all 94 judicial districts and to create one criminal debt database to provide current and comprehensive information on the payment of criminal debt.

Parenthetically, I would add, this is a way of resolving the current fragmentation among the three different local agents. The Fine Center was originally scheduled to be operational nationwide in early 1995, but it has been delayed. The project proved to be more complex and difficult than envisioned. And as a result, the Administrative Office has now redesigned the project by adopting a new two-part implementation plan. Implementation of the first part began in April of this year. And its objective is to develop and operate a basic billing, collection, disbursing and accounting processing center and to convert all 94 district courts to this central system by September 1996.

According to Administrative Office officials, this first part will produce a manual system in which clerks of court, probation offices, and U.S. Attorney offices submit hard copies of criminal debt accounting records to the Administrative Office. The Administrative Office will then computerize the data on a system here in Washington. During implementation of the first phase, the Administrative Office expects to procure and enhance an automated system which it expects to be in place within 5 years.

According to the Justice Department, as you also mentioned earlier, outstanding criminal debt grew from $.3 billion to $3.6 billion between fiscal years 1985 and the end of fiscal year 1993, and has now, as we understand it, actually reach $4 billion. Much of this increase is attributable to penalties imposed and financial institution fraud cases. For example, almost half of the total criminal debt balance is owed by offenders sentenced in major bank and thrift basis. The vast majority of this is a form of restitution orders and fines.

How much of the outstanding debt is realistically collectible and how effectively are agencies collecting criminal debts, it is very difficult to tell because of severe data limitations and other factors. The Government now lacks complete and reliable data on criminal debt balances. Both the courts and the Justice Department maintain some data on outstanding debt, but for a variety of reasons, their data may not agree.

For example, during our earlier review of the National Fine Center, we noted that it took over a year to reconcile differing balances for one judicial district's 2,500 accounts. The data also is incomplete. For example, the systems do not indicate the terms of the fine or restitution orders. Depending upon how the orders are worded, offenders may owe nothing until the last day of supervised release. A problem related to that is that, as I mentioned earlier, some restitution orders may be payable directly to the victims. It is very hard in the system now to track and account for restitution payments that are made directly to victims without any intervention by one of the Federal agents.

As a result of these problems, no one is able to determine with any certainty how much is due and how much has been collected. The fragmentation of collection responsibility and lack of reliable comprehensive data also means that the Federal Government cannot assure that debtors who do not pay are quickly identified and pursued. These problems are likely to persist in our view until the National Fine Center is fully operational.

Even if comprehensive information were available, however, it may still be difficult to evaluate how much criminal debt the Government should realistically expect to collect. The Attorney General testified in 1990 that only about 5 to 10 percent of losses in financial institution fraud cases may be recovered through civil and criminal proceedings. Justice believed that there was little or nothing left to collect or recover at the conclusion of the criminal process in many cases when sentencing occurs.

Additionally, Justice has pointed out that Federal courts tended to base their restitution orders and financial institution fraud cases more on the amount of loss to the victims than on the offenders current ability to pay. According to Justice, this created an inevitable gap between the amounts owed and the amounts collected. Justice maintains that the collection rates in these cases is not unexpectantly low because historically it is only realistic to expect that a small fraction of the total losses will be recovered.

On the other hand, in a study of 59 financial institution fraud cases, Justice found that its collection rate rose to over 30 percent, ones that accounted for debt that was legally uncollectible, either because the debt had been appealed or was not due until the offender was on probation. Justice pointed out, and we certainly agree, that a truly accurate picture of its collection efforts requires further consideration of the offender's financial condition and present and future capacity to pay fines and restitution.

Justice has taken some actions to improve criminal debt collection. For example, U.S. Attorneys have implemented criminal debt management plans that focus on the identification and active enforcement of collectible, criminal debt. Also, Justice is working with the Resolution Trust Corporation and the Federal Deposit Insurance Corporation to establish better procedures to identify, reconcile, prioritize and develop collection strategies for financial institution fraud debts.

These are positive steps. However, we believe that several areas merit further review and continued oversight. Foremost among these in our view is the National Fine Center. As I mentioned earlier, until the Fine Center is operational on a national basis, criminal debt collection efforts will continue to be hampered by the lack of fundamental information on balances due and collected. Considering the difficulties that the Administrative Office has encountered in developing the system over the past several years and the very recent fundamental change in approach, we believe that further implementation of the Fine Center project is an area that deserves continued oversight.

Second, in our work on bank and thrift fraud, we were told about the importance of identifying suspects' assets early on during investigation before the assets can be moved or dissipated. Recently Justice has acknowledged that efforts to identify assets could be enhanced, particularly in the context of forfeiture. That is another major area we think deserves additional attention is the amount of effort and the capacity of law enforcement officials to identify and locate assets that could be seized, forfeited or otherwise used to meet criminal debt collection obligation.

This concludes my summary statement, Mr. Chairman. I will be happy to answer any questions.

Senator DORGAN. Mr. Wray, I am cognizant of the fact that much of this increase in fines and restitution orders results from massive fraud in financial institutions in the last 10 years and the substantial amount from the savings and loan industry which some bilked the institution, and subsequently the taxpayers, of billions of dollars. And the taxpayers ended up having to make it good through the bailout. The American people would expect that those who committed that fraud would be slapped with a heavy fine of restitution, would lose what they have, with a sense of failure.

This picture that you paint of the management of the collection of fines and restitution orders makes it sound like it is decentralized, ineffective and pretty much a mess. The fines have increased from 1986 to now over tenfold, $300 million to nearly $4 billion or as you say just over $4 billion. It seems to me the method for collecting it is a mess. Is that a way to summarize your report?

Mr. WRAY. There certainly are a lot of problems of various kinds. I think certainly we recognize that it is going to be challenging to collect a lot of debt, particularly in these cases under the best of circumstances. But we believe that major efforts could be undertaken now to do our best to at least better identify and pursue that debt which does appear to be collectible.

Senator DORGAN. Let me ask you some questions about a couple of points you made. You made one point about—in the construction of a National Fine Center in trying to reconcile what is going on. You said it took over 1 year to reconcile 2,500 accounts. You were talking about the disarray here of this system. How on earth can that happen?

Mr. WRAY. The fact is that this flows largely from the decentralized way in which the payments are accounted for now, both entities within the judicial branch and the Justice Department maintain information on debts, but we found that it often did not agree. There were differences in terms of how much was owed and the massive effort in this one Federal judicial district simply to arrive at totals in terms of what the Government thought was owed in these cases.

Senator DORGAN. But how would that take a year? It seems to me if you assigned someone the responsibility to do that, you would get that done. I understand that somewhere around 30 to 36 percent of those who owe fines and restitutions, there is no address for them. And I assume most of these folks are on some kind of supervised probation or some system in the criminal justice system that keeps track of them. And yet for purposes of collecting fines and restitution orders, about a third of them are not able to be located; is that correct?

Mr. WRAY. I might ask Mr. Martin who worked on our earlier review to elaborate on our finding.

Mr. MARTIN. That is correct, Mr. Chairman. In the Eastern District of North Carolina, they were unable to locate about 36 percent of the criminal debtors. We understand from the people in the courts down there that that sort of situation arose there part because the probation officers were under a tremendous workload. They were probably concentrating more on offenders who presented more of a violent danger to the community rather than debtors from several years ago and they lost track of them.

Senator DORGAN. So the task of actually collecting a fine or restitution order becomes an afterthought and it is assigned to people who have other duties or may have other duties and it has not under the decentralized system been a set of circumstances where this is a focus. You say all right if part of the penalty in the criminal justice system is to levy a fine or a restitution order, then we have to effect that penalty. And as I hear your description of the system, it looks like once you've got a guilty plea and you've made the assessment of the penalty or the fine or the sentence rather, then it sort of becomes an afterthought of whether it ever gets collected under this system.

Mr. WRAY. Justice itself has recognized that the incentives are somewhat mixed and then priorities, obviously the individuals and the courts and then the Justice Department have a lot of priorities and a lot of competing objectives, but that collection, as Justice has suggested in a recent report, may not be a high priority among assistant U.S. Attorneys and others who do their jobs fundamentally as putting crooks in jail and that collection does not quite rise to the same level of significance an their eyes. That is understandable in a sense that that is what they are there to do, but we think that greater priority could be given to debt collection efforts.

Senator DORGAN. I understand that there criminal fines imposed against those who have been convicted that will never ever be collectible. I mean I understand that because these are folks who have nothing. They are never going to have anything. You can throw them in jail; let them out. The fact is, they are never going to be able to pay anything. But that is reflected in the $300 million that was owed back in 1986. There is a continuing level of those miscellaneous, relatively small Federal fines that you assess because you should assess them as a penalty but that we are not going to collect. Understand that and accept that.

We have seen the growth tenfold of fines and restitution orders. In most cases, very large fines, very large restitution orders against some of the more significant criminals in the last decade or two in this country's history. They did not use guns. They used pencils and they held up the American taxpayer for billions of dollars and are now fined or ordered to pay restitution, many of whom are essentially paying nothing.

And as I read the description of the system, because we do not have a centralized system, the method of extracting this penalty from those criminals is not extracting very much, maybe a penny on a dollar. It offends me and I would expect offends most of the American people to see a penny on a dollar collected from fines assessed on some of the highest rollers who corrupted and defrauded the S&L industry in the 1980's.

Mr. WRAY. That certainly is a problem. One thing I might just mention in regard to that is the way the priorities work in the system. A restitution orders have a higher priority by law than collecting fines. In the case of most of the S&L cases, the vast amounts of uncollected debt are in the form of restitution and that presumably, the emphasis would be on doing what one can to collect that, as opposed to the fines. But that is right.

And in fact, one, this may be a fairly modest step, but one step the Justice has suggested and that we think would be a good idea, is once we get a handle on these outstanding balances, try to do a better job of segregating those debts that do seem to offer some reasonable prospect for collection. And then to sort of put the other ones in a different category and concentrate what limited efforts we do have on the ones that are more likely to be collected.

Senator DORGAN. That is why one asks the question, what is achievable here? Is it 5 percent or 10 percent or much more or much less? We do not have any idea, because the system itself is so poor that you cannot even assess what you might achieve with a good system.

I want to ask some questions about the National Fine Center. $19 million was made available to establish a National Fine Center. That money came from the Victims Fund, as I understand it?

Mr. WRAY. That is correct.

Senator DORGAN. That comes out of the money that would otherwise be in the Victims Fund. $5 million of that has now been spent. We have no National Fine Center at this point. And I want you to elaborate on the question, have they in effect suspended the work that was done with the $5 million to go in another direction? And if so, what on earth did they do with the $5 million?

Mr. WRAY. The $5 million was used for hardware, software purposes and primarily for a number of other—salaries and other expenses to fund the initial pilot project approach that they used over the last few years. Again, maybe Mr. Martin can elaborate on where the money has gone.

Senator DORGAN. I will ask the question to later witnesses, but I am trying to understand from you, you all have been in to look at that. We said we want a National Fine Center. We made money available for that. Five of the $19 million has been spent. And now you are telling me that a new system, a new approach, is now undertaken with a two-step process, the first step of which will be a manual system. What on earth does that mean? I mean I do not understand this. What has $5 million been spent for, if we now have a new approach with a two-step process, the first stage of which will be a manual system?

Mr. Martin.

Mr. MARTIN. Senator, we have done relatively limited work on what the courts have done since the Raleigh effort. Our understanding from meeting with the courts and reviewing documents that they provided to us, generally is they are regarding the $5 million as having been an investment in learning what they can and cannot do in a rapid, ineffective way. We do not know at this point exactly what lessons they learned from the district of North Carolina that have been applied to current efforts.

Senator DORGAN. Would it be hard for you to do some more analysis of how the $5 million was spent? I mean it is not exactly rocket science to collect. I ran an agency, a fairly large agency, in which we had a collection section and we had a lot of collectors. This is not rocket science at all. This is the most fundamental of administrative duties to know what is the population you are collecting from? What are your rights? How do you go about it? What kind of system do you have? Do you automate it? If so, how? I am just trying to understand if you spent $5 million and are now going to have a new system, the first stage of which is manual, what on earth happened to the money?

Mr. WRAY. As I understand it fundamentally they embarked on sort of a very elaborate state-of-the-art system initially. It is possible that they bit off more than they could chew and then went for a more elaborate system that could practically be put in place. And then perhaps greatly underestimated the complexity of the system they were putting in place. That is why the first stage of the revised plan, as I understand it, is really designed just to get some basic information into the system to enable us to at least get a start on this, rather than initially trying for the state-of-the-art system.

Senator DORGAN. Having looked at this issue in its broadest terms, what kind of recommendations would you give to Congress at this point? We have now been down the road a good number of years after which we decided we want a National Fine Center. We now find ourselves well down the road, having $5 million spent and now a new system with a two-step process to be implemented, the first stage of which will be implemented 2 years and 3 or 4 months from now. Should we have confidence that in September 1996, the first stage of that will be implemented, even manually? And if so, why should we have that confidence?

Mr. WRAY. I think we would recommend certainly that the implementation of the system in the next couple of years be given intense scrutiny. I think, obviously in light of the problems they have had in the past, one would want to be optimistic at the present time. In addition, there are other areas that we think probably deserve particular attention. For example, the security of the computer system is going to be a very important factor in the Fine Center and we are not sure how that fits into the current planning.

Another issue is it is not clear to us at this moment whether the new system will just start accumulating information on new criminal debt or how we are going to go back and bring in the debt that is outstanding now or try to reconcile that. I think those are two particular issues that occur to us at the present time. But I think more generally the implementation of the Fine Center will require considerable oversight.

Senator DORGAN. Are you familiar with other collection system in the public and private sector? I mean we are filled with credit cards in our society and we have collections going on for both the

80-935 - 95 - 2

private and public sector for a wide range of activities. Are you generally familiar with how those work?

Mr. WRAY. I cannot say that I am an expert in those in the system, no.

Senator DORGAN. I am just wondering how this system—I am guessing that a large credit card company could not conceivably operate with this kind of a collection system. Any observations?

Mr. WRAY. I would assume that that is correct. Obviously they are faced with very different challenges and somewhat different clientele than we are dealing with here, but certainly I am sure there must be many lessons to be learned from those experiences. Part of the Fine Center was actually modeled on the Central Violations Bureau that we have.

Senator DORGAN. It might be some of the same clientele now that we think about it.

Mr. WRAY. That is possible also. But there are Central Violations Bureaus, I think, in two courts of the country now that handle debt, relatively minor debt, that arises from crime on Federal property and that has provided some examples.

Senator DORGAN. I guess what we would like to do is have the GAO conduct some additional oversight for us between now and September of 1996, and I would also like to inquire if I could get some information about how the $5 million was spent.

Mr. WRAY. We can submit something for the record.

Senator DORGAN. I will be glad to send you an inquiry and ask if we can, without extensive work, try and understand what has happened to that. I mean it may well be that it is an investment that is embodied in future systems and it may also be that somebody tried to set up the most elaborate system in the world because they were using money from the Victims Fund, and the fact is $5 million may have been frittered away. But I guess that is a question for others and probably for another day.

Mr. WRAY. We would be happy to look into that.

Senator DORGAN. Senator McCain has submitted a series of questions which I will submit as well. He asks one question that touches on something I alluded to. We have vast numbers of private sector organizations which have substantial experience in integrated debt management and collection systems and Senator McCain asks whether you have seen instances in which a discussion was held to contract some of this collection for fines and restitutions by the private sector? We will submit these questions.

One other question, I think you probably have not had a chance to look indepth at this. The Federal Government has a number of devices to apply pressure to those who owe them money and the filing of liens and a range of other things, some of which everybody in the country has as remedies, and the Federal Government has some other more unique remedies. Because the system is so chaotic and so fragmented, is there any way for you to assure us that the folks who are in charge of collecting that debt at the district level are aggressive and filing liens when necessary and doing the kinds of things that one would expect a creditor to do to protect themselves?

Mr. WRAY. Our impression from the work we have done, and we have not looked intensively at this in very recent times, is that the people, particularly in the U.S. Attorney's office, Financial Litigation Unit, attorneys are working very aggressively to collect the debt within the limits of their resources. However, the relatively few attorneys assigned to this task in the U.S. Attorney's office, and again Justice itself in a September 1993 inspector general report indicated that there are some problems with information sharing, for example, between the prosecuting assistant U.S. Attorneys and the attorneys in the office who are charged with collecting criminal debt. That is an area that the IG thought could be improved.

The IG also found that interest and penalties were not being assessed on delinquent debt in some cases. So there are various steps that can be taken to enhance collection efforts, even given the current information problems. A lot of it really comes down to a question of priority and then competing resources. U.S. Attorneys are undoubtedly faced with an awful lot of competing demands and that collection may not be very high in that list of priorities.

Senator DORGAN. Give me an example of a district. With a couple of hundred of attorneys in the U.S. Attorney's office, I understand maybe two of them are assigned the responsibility for collection? Would that be an example that is——

Mr. MARTIN. I would not say that that is out of line, Senator. It is hard to tell in particular districts at any given point in time, but I know that having been in the Southern District of Florida, Miami, which is one of the larger U.S. Attorney offices in the country, that there may be, may be, two assistant U.S. Attorneys that work in the Financial Litigation Unit and then a couple of paralegal, financial analysts. Out of maybe 100 people total in the office, four or five financial litigation. I know that Justice Department people could tell you much better.

Senator DORGAN. The reason this is important is part of getting tough with respect to those that commit this fraud, especially in financial restitution fraud, part of getting tough is not just assessing a fine, but requiring it to be paid, to the extent that the defendant has the capability of paying it. If you have got circumstances as we see, where the system is so fragmented and where in the districts where you have got a lot of criminal activity, most of the attorneys are off working on that and the collection is an afterthought, you might well prefer to owe the money to the U.S. Justice Department than a credit card company, because it will be a lot less hassle from the Justice Department based on this kind of a system.

Mr. WRAY. We have also found, we have done some work on civil debt collection also, and we found that even on the civil side debt collection tends not to be a real high priority. In fact, Justice has experimented in a number of districts with actually contracting out civil debt to private attorneys and they have had some success with that. That might be a possibility for consideration in some of the restitution areas and some of the criminal areas. Although I think the Government would have to be very careful with firms, on whether that is a good approach. But there are problems on the civil side also.

Senator DORGAN. We would like, Mr. Wray, for the GAO to do some additional work for us in the coming 2 years, so that we can track the progress of the National Fine Center. We are making a significant investment in that and we would expect the investment would pay off. I think the American people would expect those who are assessed fines, especially the type I have mentioned, would be required to pay some of those fines to the extent they are able to do so.

I want to thank you for updating your 1993 information and I would hope that in the coming months we can work together on some of these issues and watch between now and September of 1996 what progress we make on the National Fine Center. Thank you very much for appearing today, Ms. Montgomery and Mr. Martin. And Mr. Wray, thank you very much.

We would like to ask the next panel to come forward. Mr. Richard Ames, the Assistant Director for Finance and Budget, the U.S. Administrative Office of the Courts; accompanied by Mr. Peter G. McCabe and Ms. Nancy Fleetwood. Mr. McCabe is the Assistant for Judges Programs and Ms. Nancy Fleetwood is the Chief, Accounting and Financial Systems Division.

The other person on this panel is Mr. Gerald M. Stern, Special Counsel, Financial Institution Fraud, the Department of Justice. Mr. Stern is accompanied by Mr. Richard Sponseller, the Deputy Director of the Executive Office of the U.S. Attorneys.

While they are coming forward, I would like to indicate that we are including in a record a statement by our colleague, Harris Wofford, who is interested in this issue, who has done some work on this issue and that will be made a part of the hearing record.[1]

Senator DORGAN. Mr. Ames, thank you for being with us today. Mr. Ames, you may proceed. Your entire statement will be made a part of the permanent record, and you're able to summarize it, as you wish.

TESTIMONY OF RICHARD A. AMES,[2] ASSISTANT DIRECTOR FOR FINANCE AND BUDGET, U.S. ADMINISTRATIVE OFFICE OF THE COURTS, ACCOMPANIED BY PETER G. McCABE, ASSISTANT DIRECTOR FOR JUDGES PROGRAMS, AND NANCY C. FLEETWOOD, CHIEF, ACCOUNTING AND FINANCIAL SYSTEMS DIVISION

Mr. AMES. Thank you, Senator Dorgan, and thank you for the opportunity to be here to report on the status of the National Fine Center. We really appreciate your support and your interest in this extremely important project.

Before starting, I comment briefly on my background. I joined the Administrative Office on January 31 of this year and had the opportunity to take on this project on April 26. Before coming to the Federal Government, I had spent 28 years in the private sector at Ford Motor Company and Union Pacific Railroad, where I was Chief, Financial Officer. This subject and these topics are not new to me.

I would also like to take the opportunity to introduce my colleague, Nancy Fleetwood. Nancy, as you know, is Chief of our Accounting and Financial Systems Division. And she and I together are taking the lead with this cross functional, cross branch, cross

[1] See on page 49.
[2] The prepared statement of Mr. Ames appears on page 49.

agency effort to bring the National Fine Center project to completion. Nancy's background and experience is very relevant. She has 15 years of experience in the Federal Government, primarily with Treasury, and she has implemented similar systems in the past. So we bring experience to this project.

Nancy I share your sense of urgency. We are working hard to make this happen. We consider this our highest priority and we know our director considers it one of the eight Administrative Office's highest priorities.

Turning now to the status of the Fine Center project. First the financial status. We have spent $5.7 million to date of the $19 million appropriated. The $5.7 million went primarily as follows: $2.7 million for salaries and benefits; $1.5 million for equipment; $1 million for contractor services; and $500,000 for a variety of other expenses like telephones, travel, supplies.

From an implementation plan viewpoint, the key point is that we have completed our planning and development stage. That was completed on April 26. At that point, we began the implementation stage and the baton was passed to Nancy and myself. We have two-step plan—a basic system and an enhanced system. The basic system plan is within the first 120 days, starting from April 26, by August 26, to have completed all the startup efforts and to have the first court up and running. Within the next 242 days, we would add 22 more courts, for a total of 23 courts at the end of the first year from April 26. And all 94 courts would be up by August 26 of 1996 which would be 2 years from the first court being up.

The initial basic system is not a manual system, but rather a partially automated system. We will be using software which we have selected. We will be working on, during this period that I described, between now and September of 1996, to enhance this basic system as we go. The interfaces, whether they be input from the court units or information transferred to Treasury or to the Department of Justice or to the Bureau of Prisons, will be automated and converted to electronic transmission during this period. The main thing that we will not have during the initial process is immediate on-line access by all customers. That will come in the second enhanced fees.

The enhanced system will take longer to develop, but the important point here, I think, is we just want to do it after a planning stage that took longer than any of us wanted or expected when we started. So in effect, we have adopted that motto, "Just Do It" and we are focusing on getting these courts up just as quickly as we can and enhancing this initial system to start with. There were a lot of lessons learned. We believe that a lot of value was received for the initial $5.7 million and that relates to the planning and development process that was pursued. A key part of that was the prototype operation in Raleigh.

Some of the difficulties that we experienced early that brought us difficulty was that frankly we were too easy. Our basis initial approach was to go out and work with the various court units, totalling almost 300, and with the Department of Justice and the Bureau of Prisons and RTC and FDIC, and even OMB, as various of these activities showed an interest in the Fine Center project. And our strategy was, let us find out what our customers need and let us meet those needs. By the time we finished, one of the key things we learned from the Raleigh prototype was that that grand design was much too grand, would take way too many dollars and way too much time to complete.

Senator DORGAN. But where did the grand design proposal come from? Where did that originate?

Mr. AMES. It came out of this planning and development process where the Administrative Office worked with all of the users, including the various court users, as well as the other agencies that we were working with. And we said, what do you need from this Fine Center project? Other things, examples of things that we encountered that turned out to be overly ambitious were the Judgment and Commitment Statement which is a key part of court proceedings and records the basic terms of the sentence and we found that that varied a lot from court to court.

But initially people thought it was important to automate that, so we begged into the Fine Center project initially, automating the J&C statement. That turned out to be a project that is extremely difficult to achieve and one that would and could delay the Fine Center for a long time.

You and others alluded earlier to the difficulty with reconciling the accounts. That is a huge problem and a lot of time and effort went into doing that and that again turned out to be a key reason for delay. And in each of those cases, whether it is developing a grander system than perhaps is really needed, certainly in the short-term; whether it is to automate the J&C; whether it is to reconcile all of the accounts, if we made all of those in the end preconditions, things that had to happen before we could have the Fine Center, it will take a very long time.

So that is why we came up with this modified plan that starts out with the basic system. And the easiest way to think about it is why do we not get a Ford Falcon up and running with a grander plan to end up down the road with a Lincoln Continental with all of the options and electronics that anyone could ever conceive. But let us get the basic system in place and running. And that is what came out of the Raleigh process since April 26. On this timetable we have established, we are on target and we are committed to achieving the objectives. We have a sense of urgency and we are committed to get a return on this investment.

Senator DORGAN. I will ask Mr. Stern to proceed momentarily, but I notice his examples of automobiles, they are all Fords.

Mr. AMES. Yes, sir, 22 years of training.

Senator DORGAN. Let me just ask two questions, then I will come back and we will ask Mr. Stern. You talk about reconciling accounts, a massive job. A year to reconcile 2,500 accounts, that ought not be a massive job; should it be?

Mr. AMES. I am not familiar with the 2,500 number. That sounds lower than I would have expected. But the account reconciliation problem is substantial, as alluded to by the gentleman from GAO. And that relates to different approaches within each of the three court units and a lack of uniformity among the 94 courts and those units, each unit not tracking the same thing, the same way, and the same time period. And it is further exacerbated by changes in the sentences which can happen and that is an important differentiator from the department store example.

Senator DORGAN. I am going to ask you a series of questions, but I will defer until we have heard from the other panel member. I would observe that someone once said that if you were to order a television set from the Pentagon, it would cost at least $100,000 to $200,000 for them to build it, because they would immediately begin creating design specs for how they wanted a television set built. The same is true with respect to creating a National Fine Center.

I am very interested in having a computer list of all felons in this country done on an urgent, national priority and done quickly. I had all the people in my office from the FBI and Justice, you know a room full of 12, and I almost after an hour, wanted to kick them all out. It was so frustrating, because you simply could not talk about what is necessary to do the simple task of putting on a computer list, a national database of felons. And I am expecting that that is probably part of the problem you have when you say, let us create a National Fine Center and you get 10 people in the room who think, largely bureaucratically, of what this must be from their standpoint. First when you get a system that is Rube Goldberg like, sort of Byzantine that probably cannot be built.

I am going to come back and ask a series of questions about that. I appreciate your testimony and let me now ask Mr. Stern, special counsel, Financial Institution Fraud, Department of Justice. Mr. Stern, would you proceed?

Before I do that, let me welcome Senator Cohen and ask if he has an opening statement?

Senator COHEN. I do have an opening statement and I would like to submit it for the record.

PREPARED STATEMENT OF SENATOR COHEN

Mr. Chairman, I would like to commend you and Senator Dorgan for holding this hearing today to examine the Federal Government's collection of criminal debt.

Specifically, the Committee will examine why the Department of Justice has failed to collect more than $3.6 billion in outstanding criminal fines and restitution. Unfortunately, this is a longstanding problem. Over the last decade there have been a number of congressional, General Accounting Office (GAO), and Inspector General (IG) reviews of the government's failure to collect outstanding criminal debt. In addition, Congress passed two major legislative initiatives to address this problem—in 1984, Congress passed the Criminal Fine Enforcement Act and in 1987, the Criminal Fine Improvements Act.

Despite numerous reports and legislative efforts which stressed the need to increase the efficiency and enforcement of Federal criminal fines and restitution, the balance of outstanding debt continues to grow at an alarming pace. For example, in fiscal year 1985, the amount of unpaid criminal debt totaled $260 million. By fiscal year 1989, that figure had grown to $968 million and today it stands in excess of $3.6 billion—an almost 14 fold increase over the last decade.

A large portion—about 47 percent—of this uncollected debt can be traced to fines and restitution assessed to those whose criminal actions involved financial institutions including the savings and loan failures. For example, it seems that Charles Keating and his son, who made millions as they presided over the loss of $2.5 billion in Lincoln assets and were both convicted of financial institution fraud, have yet to pay a dime of the $220 million in court-ordered restitution. The Justice Department is currently taking action to recover a number of Keating-related assets.

Non-S&L-related criminals have also paid little or nothing in the form of fines and restitution. For example, in two drug-related cases in New York and Illinois where fines totalled about $75 million, the government has collected a total of $425.

In a letter to the Justice Department's Inspector General, the Department itself acknowledged that criminal debt is not effectively collected. However, just as we are outraged when criminals escape from prison, we should feel equally outraged if criminals escape from other sanctions such as failing to pay their fines and restitution. We must be certain that criminals pay their *entire* debt to society.

Today's hearing will shed light on why the government has not been able to collect these debts. I would caution that there is more here than meets the eye. Admittedly there are some cases where convicted criminals may indeed be unable to pay, however, the government's inability to collect criminal fines and restitution may be linked to sophisticated practices of successfully hiding assets from the government. According to published reports, the FBI estimates that $300 billion in illegal profits are successfully hidden from the scrutiny of U.S. law enforcement officials every year.

Over the past decade, Congress has strengthened the ability of the government to seize assets used in the commission of crimes. We in Congress have also emphasized the use of criminal fines to ensure that the felons' wallets also feel the effects of their illegal activities. Additionally, Congress has requested that the U.S. Attorneys and the Administrative Office of the U.S. Courts work together to increase collections of outstanding criminal debt by establishing the National Fine Center to track and account for outstanding criminal fines and restitution. The latter effort was passed by Congress in 1987. Yet for the past 7 years, the Administrative Office of the U.S. Courts and the Justice Department have dragged their collective feet and failed to properly coordinate their efforts. Consequently, the National Fine Center is not yet a reality and billions of dollars in criminal fines and restitution is going uncollected.

I hope that this hearing will encourage the Administrative Office of the U.S. Courts and the Justice Department to recognize the importance these collection efforts have—especially to victims of crime. If the Administrative Office of the U.S. Courts and the Justice Department do not act promptly to resolve this lack of coordination, they can expect additional legislation to resolve this issue.

Hopefully, the testimony we hear today will assist the Committee in developing a plan to ensure that outstanding criminal debt is realistically assessed and collected. I look forward to hearing the testimony of our witnesses.

Senator DORGAN. Without objection. Mr. Stern, why do you not proceed.

TESTIMONY OF GERALD M. STERN,[1] SPECIAL COUNSEL, FINANCIAL INSTITUTION FRAUD, DEPARTMENT OF JUSTICE, ACCOMPANIED BY RICHARD W. SPONSELLER, DEPUTY DIRECTOR, EXECUTIVE OFFICE FOR UNITED STATES ATTORNEYS

Mr. STERN. Thank you, Senator Dorgan, Senator Cohen. I am the Department of Justice's Special Counsel for Financial Institution Fraud and the Attorney General has also asked me to oversee the Department's efforts in debt collection, and as you indicated, some of the Financial Institution Fraud orders are a large part of the Department's and Government's debt collection numbers. We appreciate this opportunity to provide the Committee with the Department's comments on its debt collection efforts.

We believe there has been significant collection of outstanding debt and restitution orders in the Financial Institution Fraud cases, but all recoveries with respect to the defendants covered by those orders are considered. The Department's efforts to pursue the losses in the S&L cases and the other Federal Financial Institution Fraud crimes begin not merely at the time the court orders the defendant to pay restitution for a fine or a special assessment, those orders come at the end of the line. Our efforts begin much earlier in pursuing the lost assets and recovering the fraud losses from the beginning that we start to work on the case.

[1] The prepared statement of Mr. Stern appears on page 65.

In March 1994, we analyzed all the FDIC and RTC cases involving outstanding restitution orders of over $1 million. We had to do this basically on a manual approach but we did it. The sum of all the recoveries to satisfy these $1 million and over cases, which by the way accounted for about 90 percent of all the outstanding FDIC and RTC restitution orders, the sum of all our recoveries there, is approximately $245 million or approximately 31 percent of the total order. This is a good record, particularly when you remember that the restitution orders themselves are based on the lost caused by the defendant rather than on the defendant's ability to pay.

However, as the GAO's testimony indicated earlier today, many of these orders involved defendants who are still in jail. Senator Dorgan, your reference to the top 50 criminal debts owed to the United States is a survey that I put together and provided to your staff earlier in the year and which the GAO has now had a chance to review. You look at each of those 50 and you can tell where they are. We have their addresses. Basically most of them are in jail.

You can also see that although the actual dollar recovery on the restitution order is very low as you pointed out, properly pointed out, the actual amount recovered from these 50 people was quite high. I think the total amount of the order, for example, the range of $834 million, the actual amount paid on the order through the system would have been $4.1 million. But if you look at the forfeitures and other recoveries that we had with respect to these defendants as the system began, rather than look at the very end, we had over $219 million in recoveries.

If I can point to one specific example which I think explains one of the difficulties we are having here, Mr. Keating and his son account for one-quarter of a billion dollars of the restitution orders for these top 50 people. They are, in fact, No. 1 and 2 on the list. That one-quarter of a billion dollars is a large part of the $834 million. If you look at how much has been paid by them on the actual restitution orders, it is zero. But if you look at how much has been recovered from them, $111 million was obtained by the RTC from the sale of the hotel interest that they had. There are other efforts still outstanding if you try and trace down any assets they have.

But it is a part of looking at this in terms of the restitution order at the end. We have to wait to the end to get the money. Usually the money has been dissipated. That is one of the reasons we start very early seeking asset freezes and forfeitures at the outset and try and get civil and criminal recoveries at the outset and not wait until you get the criminal conviction at the end.

With respect to the National Fine Center itself, the part of Justice recognizes that it will not be able to have full and accurate information for itself or for the Congress on outstanding criminal debt recoveries and payments until this Fine Center is fully operational. We had hoped it would be up and running by now and we have tried to provide whatever support we can to the Administrative Office of the U.S. Courts to get that particular Center up an running. I have met with them myself now that I am in this position for the Department of Justice on debt collection and I have every hope that they will be able to get this Fine Center up and running. But truthfully until it is, we have to continue to work on this manual basis that we use and which we have used in the Financial Institution Fraud area.

I have submitted a statement for the record to deal with the other questions which the Committee has asked. I would be happy to answer any questions that you have.

Senator DORGAN. Senator Cohen.

Senator COHEN. Thank you, Mr. Chairman. How would you respond to the GAO's testimony that most forfeiture proceeds are used to fund law enforcement activities and that forfeiture may divert assets and restitution? There seems to be a real split between GAO and your statement.

Mr. STERN. It is our policy that restitution come before and early, but there are certain limitations in the law with respect to that. On the civil side, we cannot give restitution payments directly to the victims unless they are victim owners. So if it is a FIREA case, there is specific statutory authority which does allow us to do it. If it is a criminal case, there is specific authority that does allow us to do it. Certain civil cases, though we are not allowed to do it.

Senator COHEN. So is it breaking down on criminal versus civil restitutions?

Mr. STERN. It is after respective FIREA where there is specific authority on the civil side for us to do that.

Senator COHEN. GAO has also testified that as a means of enforcing collection, the Justice Department encourages offenders who are currently incarcerated to participate in the Bureau of Prisons Inmate Financial Responsibility Program in order to collect some of that delinquent or defaulted debt. How much have you collected and how successful is the program?

Mr. STERN. We have collected $80 million since the inception of the program through that program. It has been very effective.

Senator COHEN. The Justice IG found that 33 percent of all criminal debts outstanding in fiscal year 1991 which they calculated would be worth an estimated $565 million were 3 years or older. The IG recommended identifying these debts as uncollectible and leaving those in the balance due. Do you think this is a good idea?

Mr. STERN. Yes, I do, and we have asked the U.S. Attorneys to provide us with the amounts which should go into a suspension account. We will get our first information on that at the end of this month. By the end of the year, everyone is supposed to be reporting to us and we expect that a substantial amount of the debt that is on there will go into a suspense, basically uncollectible category.

Senator COHEN. The Justice IG, in his September 1993 audit report on criminal debt collection efforts stated that U.S. Attorneys offices were not uniformly applying interest and penalties on criminal debts which were either delinquent or in default. What is your Department's rationale for not assessing interest and penalties on these debts?

Mr. STERN. We, in fact, sent out a notification to all the U.S. Attorneys that they are to collect interest and penalties with respect to that debt. And we believe now that we have corrected that mistake that the IG pointed out to us.

Senator COHEN. In other words, if there is not, at least the threat of some additional penalty there is very little incentive to pay the debt?

Mr. STERN. Exactly.

Senator COHEN. I have one other question. GAO estimates that about 47 percent of the $3.6 billion criminal debt balance is due to major financial institutional fraud cases. I assume that means the other half is representative of other crimes. Have the assets of the nonfinancial types of crimes been hidden or laundered? What is the difficulty in tracking down those assets?

Mr. STERN. Again, you can look at the top 50 list which has not only Financial Institution Fraud criminal debts but others, such as narcotics. The No. 3 person there was $49 million buying a narcotics case. We basically received about a million dollars that was the sale of forfeited property. We will not get much more on that fellow who is now serving 50 years in jail. We have other cases like that, RICO cases, where you will get a $25 million fine. Some of it has been obtained through particular orders, but most of that we are just not going to get.

The assumption that we all work on is that we are not—certainly we are not going to be able to find some of these assets at some point with respect to some of these criminals. They are criminals. They are the kind of people who are very devious, may have hidden assets away. So we air on the side of having a larger fine and restitution order, rather than what may be a more realistic one at the outset.

But we are now looking back at those years later and that is one of the reasons we are going to consider whether to put some of these into a suspense account. After a few years, you can say, well maybe we have not been able to find the assets. Maybe we should put them more into an uncollectible area.

Senator COHEN. If you put them into an uncollectible area, does that mean you forgo ever trying to collect them? In other words, for accounting purposes, you decide what is collectible and what is uncollectible. Does that mean you write them off the books and do not go after them at some future time should you receive information about hidden assets or laundered assets?

Mr. STERN. If we put them in a suspense account, we can always go after it.

Senator COHEN. There are certain limitations statutorily on when we can write off some of these debts. So by putting them in a suspense account, you still have the right to go after them.

Could I just ask one question, Mr. Ames? Do we really have an accurate assessment of what the outstanding criminal debt is in light of GAO's statement that the record keeping is quite fragmented? Do we know?

Mr. AMES. No, sir.

Senator COHEN. That is all I have right now.

Senator DORGAN. Let me ask a series of questions, Mr. Stern. How much of the outstanding criminal fines and restitution do you think are collectible? We have heard Justice at one point, some years ago say maybe 5 or 10 percent is collectible. We are seeing on the charts I showed that we are getting 1 or 2 or 4 percent at the most in cases. Could you give us some estimate, what in your mind is actually collectible out there?

Mr. STERN. Let me, at the moment, focus on Financial Institution Fraud where we have actually taken in a manual way to go through and look at that. Because the top 108 cases are RTC and FDIC and amount for almost 90 percent of the entire restitution orders that are out there with respect to the National Fraud. You can look at the actual 108 people. I had them do it. Manually they went to everyone of the U.S. Attorneys offices where these cases existed and we have a story which we have provided for each one of the 108 cases which actually involve 125 specific individuals. I think if you look at the stories we have given you, most of the money has been collected. It has been collected either through the original forfeitures which raises that 1 percent figure to more like a 30 percent figure. Or it has been collected through the actual effort after the fines and restitution orders have been imposed.

Senator DORGAN. Wait a second, when you talk about the 30 percent, are you talking about the civil litigation in which there is recovery through civil litigation?

Mr. STERN. Some of it may have been that way.

Senator DORGAN. By the RTC and the FDIC?

Mr. STERN. Some of it may have been that way; some of it may have been asset froze—the assets that were frozen.

Senator DORGAN. How much of it would have been through civil litigation? Would that not have been the bulk of it?

Mr. STERN. Yes.

Senator DORGAN. But are you not mixing apples and oranges here? We are talking about criminal fines and ordered restitution. And you are off talking about civil litigation. I guess I am asking you a question that is fairly specific and you are answering something I did not ask.

Mr. STERN. I apologize.

Senator DORGAN. I am just wondering, those who have been judged guilty of criminal behavior against whom a fine has been imposed and a restitution order imposed, with what success have we achieved collection, No. 1? And No. 2, what success do you expect to achieve collection? When you talk about the 30 percent, you are mixing something that I think is not germane to this question anyway. If one wants to discuss what have we achieved through all means in getting back for the taxpayers from some S&L that went belly-up, yes, then that is a germane answer. But I am talking about criminal behavior, assessed fines and restitution orders. What do you think is collectible?

Mr. STERN. Let me try and answer all three of those questions maybe together. When I said that, you have to look at what had already been collected from these people before they actually had a restitution order imposed upon them. I am basically saying to you that that tells you what you will be able to collect in the future. Because by the time they are convicted, Keating is a very good example, at the very end, there usually is no money left. We got $111 million from Keating by selling a half interest in a hotel that they had. But by the time he is then convicted at the end of the road, there is no money left, unless we can find it and trace it down which we are trying to do.

The simple answer to your question is I think you do need to look at what recoveries we had from these particular individuals before we finally get them convicted. The answer then to your question is after they are convicted, how much will we collect? The answer is usually very little. Let us take the percentages. Before Keating was convicted, and you know one-quarter of a billion dollars was added for restitution orders and criminal fines, our recovery rate was maybe 5 percent. Now you add one-quarter of a billion dollars of probably uncollectible money, our recovery rate goes down to 1 percent. It is part of our system in adding, as you said earlier in your statement, adding orders based on loss rather than based on the defendant's ability to pay.

Senator COHEN. Would you yield for a question? Is it contributing to the problem? Does the Justice Department contribute to the problem by seeking penalties that it knows it cannot collect? In other words, if you already know that most of the money is gone, and most of the assets have been recovered, why would the Department want to seek a penalty of one-quarter of a billion dollars on him? If you are not going to get it, what is the point of that? Are you saying to the criminal: Do not ever come back and start business again, because we are waiting for you?

Mr. STERN. Part of it is because that is a factor, the loss, a factor that the courts are supposed to take into consideration. If they were supposed to take into consideration only the defendant's ability to pay, that would be a different situation, but statutorily they are supposed to look at the loss as one of the factors. Second, the prosecutors feel that it is very important when we are dealing with criminals who have stolen this amount of money, that they be faced with a restitution order in that amount. So that if we do find those funds, which we continue to look for, we have an order outstanding already that allows us to take that money.

I think in the pending crime bill there is, a belief by Congress that we ought to be looking more and more to the loss based restitution order rather than to the defendant's ability to pay. So to the extent that that is the way Congress wants us to look at it, we will have large orders.

Senator COHEN. You will look bad.

Mr. STERN. We will look bad on the collection side and that is why I think it is important, Senator Dorgan, for us to look not only at the end result but what have we recovered as we went along the path before we actually got him convicted. I think you need to look at the whole picture. And I think, as you asked me earlier, that is part of my job as Special Counsel for Financial Institution Fraud. I am supposed to get recoveries of money for the Government and for the taxpayers, in addition to putting people in jail and in addition to getting large fines.

Senator DORGAN. Let me go back to the question. In order to manage this appropriately as a manager, you have got $4 billion that is owed to you, the Federal Government has—you are in charge of managing of that—how do you manage to it unless you have some notion of what to expect? Do you have an expectation of what you are going to get and then have a system in which those who are out trying to achieve collections are measured against some expectation?

I am just trying to understand how we deal with the $4 billion. You may say, as you have with Mr. Keating, essentially we got it all early through civil or through forfeiture, so there is nothing left unless we find something. Well the unless we find something is the operative question here. How do you know if anybody has anything? I think you referenced a couple of people in New York who went off on a—you did not reference it, but a news report I saw went off on a one-half a million dollar spending spree during the period of time when we were trying to achieve collections. You do not know what you have until you have the resources to pursue it and effectively try to collect it. And you have to set up some goals it seems to me.

And my question about what do you expect—5 or 10 percent, less than that, more than that is a question that relates to estimates put out earlier by Justice, that they thought only 5 or 10 percent of this was collectible. Is that still your feeling?

Mr. STERN. I think at the time they were talking, I have gone back and looked at that testimony, they were talking about what was outstanding at the time. Now we have added huge numbers, Keating being a very good example, that distorts the reality of what I think we will collect. There is no real, specific, simple answer I can give you, Senator Dorgan. I do not have at my fingertips the kind of data that we ought to have and that is one of the reasons the Fine Center is so important for us.

That is why—I traveled around the country on this issue and came back and said, I want to know individually the top people who owe over a million dollars. Let me look at those. I want to know who they are. I want to know what we are doing individually on those people. Because I discovered it amounted to 88 percent of the total amount owed in the Financial Institution Fraud area. If I could look at 108 people and deal with 88 percent of my problem, then I thought I would have some idea of saying to you and others, we are doing a good job or we are not doing a good job. I cannot give you a percentage of how much we will now cover of those 108 people with respect to the orders that are outstanding. I would think it is very small.

Senator DORGAN. Are you happy with where we are in the National Fine Center and do you think we have gotten our money's worth at this point?

Mr. STERN. No.

Senator DORGAN. Why?

Mr. STERN. Because I had thought at the time I took this particular job, the National Fine Center was going to be up and running.

Senator DORGAN. Why is it not?

Mr. STERN. It was to provide us with a computerized information with respect to all the debts owed so that we could do a better job of what we were supposed to do which is to collect the debts. We are now trying to do both. We are trying not only to find out what is owed, but trying to collect those debts once we discover they are owed. Our job is supposed to be only going out and prosecuting those who owe the money, not trying to find out how much is owed by each particular person, trying to match up the payment and all that. That is interfering with our efforts, so the answer is no. We are not satisfied.

Senator DORGAN. You have heard Mr. Ames testify today. Do you have some confidence that we are headed now toward a system that will be fixed and the system that will meet the needs that you see?

Mr. STERN. I have met with Mr. Ames now a few times. And I have great hopes and I have offered them whatever help we can give to get there. It is important to us to get there as quickly as possible. In fact, I think we had a fairly high level meeting with the Deputy Attorney General about this, because it is a very important issue for us to get the National Fine Center up and running.

Senator DORGAN. Mr. Ames, who was in charge of this before you?

Mr. AMES. John Hemond and Noel Augustin.

Senator DORGAN. When you hear stories like this, you have spent $5 million for a National Fine Center and we do not yet have a National Fine Center. It is sort of now starting to go in a different direction with the implementation date fully effective of September 1996. You start saying, well I have got to find out who has been doing this and find out how on earth they have spent that money. And then they send in somebody new from Ford Motor, extensive background in the area. What has transpired that you have come to this responsibility? Is there some understanding that those in charge previously were not moving in the right direction? Can you tell me what brought you to this job?

Mr. AMES. Yes, sir. Simply stated, we made a transition within the project development process. During the first 4 plus years, starting in 1990, we were in what we would call the planning and development phase of the project. On April 26, that was completed and the implementation stage began. In the last stages of the planning and development process, one of the conclusions that was reached, as I referred to earlier, was that we really needed to focus away from the grand design, the Lincoln Continental with all the electronics and all the options to the Ford Falcon.

The Ford Falcon in this analogy is basically an accounting and financial information system with some additional information, as well, that will permit us to receive monies, set up accounts receivable for each debtor to monitor those accounts. As debtors become delinquent or go into default, notify all those who should know about that, including the Department of Justice, as well as the probation offices around the country, to disburse the monies that we receive, and to maintain at all times an account status.

These are basically accounting functions. The planning and development team was more of a program and policy activity and appropriately so. But when the conclusion was reached in the final stages of the planning and development process that the Ford Falcon would be the first step, that it would have a functional orientation, it made complete sense then to pass the baton to those with the functional background, experience and expertise in developing and then implementing this kind of system, and that is what was done. So it was a very logical transition.

Senator DORGAN. Do you feel confident at this point that if we hold another hearing a year from now and 2 years from now that we will be meeting the expectations of the National Fine Center? Do you not agree that this thing has dragged on an interminable amount of time and one wonders with the explosion and fines invested around $300 million to over $4 billion, why we cannot do something relatively simple like create a National Fine Center to automate this information and go at it like managers should?

Mr. AMES. I heard two questions, Senator. Question one we will say would be the question about, do I think that this took too long? And the answer to that question is, yes I do. I think all those involved, whether they be from the Administrative Office or outside, are disappointed that it has taken as long as it has to get to this stage. The good news is that a lot was learned. Relatively good news is that although the law was passed in 1987, the planning and development process has been underway for somewhat slightly over 4 years, as opposed to 7. And that relates in part to the funding which first came in the 1990 fiscal year. But it should not have taken, certainly with hindsight, 4 plus years to get this far. And in a way, it is reminiscent of the point you were making earlier when you talked about the frustration you had in dealing with a wide variety of activities with differing interests.

But the Raleigh prototype effort turned out to be highly valuable and we could have easily gone farther faster. Farther does not necessarily mean toward the objective. It just means we could have had a lot more activity earlier in the project and sustained a high level of activity without results other than to have spent a lot more money than we have. So I think there was a good judgment made along the way, as we learned these lessons from the Raleigh effort to decide what path we wanted to follow and then commit to making that path happen.

And that leads us into your second question which is a year from now, 2 years from now, would I expect to be here and be able to testify that we are on target? And I say to that, you bet. That is our objective. That is our commitment. One of the things we did early on in our meeting with the Deputy Attorney General was lay out front and center a very simple schedule which said, this is how many courts we are going to bring on board in the initial system and when we were going to do it, very clear cut schedule.

Absolutely no one will have any question of what it is we are committing to do and no one will have any trouble determining, did we do it? And our objective is to do it, not to come back with a strong set of explanations on why we did not get there. We want to do it. We agree with you that it is important and we are dedicated to make it happen.

Senator COHEN. There actually were two questions in that, Mr. Chairman. You asked whether or not he would be here to say that they now have one on-line in 1995 and 1996? The first question was will you be here in 1995 and 1996? And the next question was will he be here testifying that they have solved the problem? Because one of the things we have had, as you pointed out, is a lot of personnel turbulence in the programs. So I guess the answer is you plan to be here in 1995 and 1996, as well?

Mr. AMES. Yes, with one of my major priorities being to make this happen.

Senator DORGAN. This test program was only in one district, one Federal district court, as I understand it. One wonders with the difficulty coming to grips with that as a pilot project, how on earth one takes that national? But that is a question you have to answer at this point and after a lot of years and a lot of dollars, I frankly do not have the confidence I would like to have that this is all going to happen.

Mr. AMES. I would like to address that briefly, if I may. And I would simply say that what we learned in the Raleigh prototype operation was that the grand design was impractical; that it would take much too much time and much too much money to implement. And second, unlikely that we would be able to actually implement it, having spent the time and money. And third, best strategy start with the Ford Falcon. So we are not moving forward now with the grand design which is what was tested; plus dealing with automating the judgment and commitment; plus trying to reconcile all of the old accounts that were not reconciled, is preconditions to being able to move forward.

We have set aside those things, established a new course with the idea of getting courts up quickly, getting this system underway, and implementing it across the Nation, just as quickly as possible on a much simpler design which we will enhance as we go.

Senator DORGAN. I am tempted to remind you of the Edsel, but I will not, in light of all of these automobile references. But Senator Cohen has a question.

Senator COHEN. I would like to ask one question on behalf of Senator McCain. You pointed out that the Administrative Office maintains that part of the problem for the collections is the different procedures in the courts themselves and he would like to know what we can do to ensure uniformity which will maximize the collections pending the establishment or the completion of the National Fine Center?

Mr. AMES. Would you mind repeating that question. I was listening, but I am not sure that I understood.

Senator COHEN. I will say it a bit slower then. The Administrative Office maintains that part of the problem with the collections is that you have differing procedures within the court system itself. The question is what can Congress, you, or any of us do pending the completion of the National Fine Center to maximize collections to ensure uniformity, so that we can try to maximize collections? Is there anything that can be done to get greater uniformity within the court system itself?

Mr. AMES. That is a complex question and one that I am not fully qualified to answer. On the other hand, relevant to your question, I believe, would be the thought that as part of the National Fine Center collection unit that we are establishing, we will be, in effect, establishing a uniform way of gaining input data which will cut across the court units and will be uniform across all 94 courts. So for that process which also was a challenge at the early stage, we are working to simplify that; believe we have a simplified approach that will work; and we will be testing it as we go and will have the liberty to adjust as we go. We do not have to start with a system A which is rigid and cannot be divested.

Senator COHEN. Mr. Stern, do you have anything to add to that?

Mr. STERN. I think that is a key question. I do not know the answer.

Senator COHEN. How about a key answer.

Mr. STERN. I do not know the answer to it, but there is this problem with the courts. There has to be a greater standardization.

Senator COHEN. So in other words, we have to wait at least until we have the completion of the Fine Center and it should try to establish uniformity. That will be probably the first time we can determine whether we can do that.

Mr. AMES. That is right. And an important element throughout this whole process, of course, is the training which happens in two arenas. One arena is here in the National Fine Center collection unit and the staff that will be doing the collection work. The other training is throughout the Federal Court system. So right now, for example, during this first 120 days, one of our many objectives during that period was to identify which court would be the first court and then to work with that court and the three key units there to reach an understanding of how the court operations will interface with the Fine Center collection unit.

Senator DORGAN. Thank you, Senator Cohen. Mr. Stern, will you at some point, when you have a Fine Center up and operating, have some expectations of what is collectible? What is troubling me here is the inability to understand what you think is collectible? What is achievable? How else would you measure progress? You have $4 billion that is owed.

How do you measure whether we are making progress? How do you measure whether you have got a bunch of folks out there working who accomplish zero and who are having lunch half the day and doing nothing, or a bunch of folks who are aggressive and finding what they should find and achieving the collection?

Mr. STERN. There are a number of ways. I think I said earlier that we have asked the U.S. Attorneys to provide us partly at the end of June, the rest by the end of this year, what orders should be put in the suspense for that $4 billion. The assumption is that at the end of this year, we will then be able to give you at least a number that looks more like a collectible number, than the number we have there now. And I think we will need some experience with that to see whether or not we collect a large percent of what we think is collectible. I think that will take us some time doing it with respect to, at least to finish the fraud areas, to be specific 108 people. Those I am following up on a daily basis. I am not finding a great collection. Some of these answers are going to be zero.

Senator DORGAN. I understand that and accept that. But on some of them, one would also expect to have an aggressive system that achieves for us what is the level we should expect. I have here, I think, the report that you have produced. I think these are the 50 names of the 50 largest fines and restitution orders and I will not go through them. You are absolutely correct that a good many of them are in jail, a few of them deceased. There are also a good many on probation or people who have been released on parole. And if you go through and look at this by name, by status, the amount ordered, date ordered, when due, the amount paid, the balance due, it is hard to draw any conclusion except that here is a list of a bunch of people who owe a lot of money to the Federal

Government who are paying nothing. Now the answer might be they have nothing.

On the other hand, could you give an assurance to the folks that live in my hometown that this bunch, many of whom committed enormous amounts of fraud and in other circumstances would be in jail much longer than the sentences reflected here, but because it was fought with a pencil, they spend less time incarcerated. Can you give us assurances that there is an aggressiveness in pursuing this, so that somebody is not out there living in the giant house, driving a brand new automobile, taking vacations, and not paying their fines and not paying their restitution? Are you confident of that? Can you give taxpayers that confidence?

Mr. STERN. Let me answer two ways. This group of 50, we have recovered, one-quarter of a billion dollars, according to the schedule given you; $219 million through forfeitures and other recoveries——

Senator DORGAN. When you say we, but that is not the Justice Department?

Mr. STERN. Oh yes, in some cases it is the Justice Department. In some cases, it is RTC. It some cases, it is FDIC.

Senator DORGAN. Of course, that is through civil litigation though; is that right?

Mr. STERN. We work together with them.

Senator DORGAN. I understand that, but that really is mixing apples and oranges. I am trying to understand the penalty that is imposed for the criminal behavior, which is the fine and the restitution order, I am trying to understand what kind of penalty that exacts from these people. Do they have resources with which they are not paying or are you confident that for the 108 you mentioned or this list of 50, that with the current system, as fragmented and decentralized as it, that we are seeking to exact that penalty from these people?

Mr. STERN. I am completely confident 108 cases, 125 people that account for about 90 percent, actually 88 percent of the entire RTC and FDIC restitution orders outstanding, we are doing absolutely everything possible to trace down any assets those people have. Because I am following it on an individual basis, person by person.

Senator DORGAN. Tell me what justifies the confidence? You are following it person by person, but with what resources? Tell me what justifies your confidence?

Mr. STERN. The Justice Department has what we call FLU units, financial litigation units, in each of the U.S. Attorneys office. That is their job to do this. In addition, the prosecutors themselves, when they work on these cases, even if they are not directly spending all of their time on a particular recovery, will spend their time on that particular defendant. And I have talked to the prosecutors. I can think of one specifically in Sacramento that I dealt with who it angered him that the man that he had then convicted, he had not gotten all the money he wanted to get from him, and he saw some indication in the newspaper that maybe this man had some money elsewhere. He kept at it. So it is not just the financial litigation unit, the individual prosecutor who prosecuted these 125 individuals, who continue to go after them.

And we also have major training exercises that we run through the Justice Department for our U.S. Attorneys, Assistant U.S. Attorneys, on this effort. And finally, the Attorney General herself has sent out a number of others to the U.S. Attorneys about her interest in continuing our efforts to recover these monies and these fines. So this is of major importance to us and I think if I may be so bold as to say, the fact that I have been asked to do this, in addition to my other job, indicates at least that we believe at the Justice Department it is important matter.

Senator DORGAN. But your desire and the practical results of that out in the field can be two different things. If you say to a district out there where they have a lot of U.S. Attorneys, but are enormously overwhelmed by the sheer amount of crime they are confronted with daily, that your priority is collection, they say, well that may be your priority sitting up there in Washington. But I tell you, we are up to our neck right here in violent crime and we do not have the foggiest intention of devoting resources to this. I am just wondering under the current fragmented system whether you have the capability to affect a good collection system out in the field?

Mr. STERN. Certainly out of 125 people, the answer is yes, I do.

Senator DORGAN. We have that list. It will be interesting that we have an enormous amount of money that has been ordered to be paid in Federal fines and restitution orders. I hope what you say is absolutely correct and I hope I will 1 day have the confidence you have that of the folks who swindled the American taxpayers have an enormous amount of money, that when fines and restitution orders are levied against them, that they are not going to retain property and assets. That their property and assets are seized to a collection of data. I would hope that all of us can have that same kind of confidence that you have.

Let me thank both of you and tell you that we intend to follow up on this. It is not my intention to try to embarrass anybody. But I want the system to work. I do not want to spend any millions of dollars on anything that is not effective. If we are going to spend millions of dollars on a National Fine Center, let us get one. Let us make it work. And let us make sure criminals pay the price for us having a National Fine Center that extracts from them the fines that have been levied, the restitution orders that have been required. That has not been the case and I hope we can change that.

Mr. Ames, we will look forward to having you come back and not having someone new show up from Chrysler or General Motors and tell us they are now going to start a new, with a new direction. We very much, all of us, want this to be fixed, to succeed, so that we do well in this area. I thank you very much for taking the time to come today and testify. We would like to submit additional questions to you that Senator McCain and others have. Thank you very much.

Next we would like to call Mr. David Beatty, the Director of Public Affairs, the National Victim Center. David, have I pronounced your last name correctly?

Mr. BEATTY. Beatty.

Senator DORGAN. David Beatty. David, you are the last witness and we would ask that your statement, which I have read, be submitted entirely for the record, and we would ask that you summarize it. Why do you not proceed.

TESTIMONY OF DAVID BEATTY,[1] DIRECTOR OF PUBLIC AFFAIRS, NATIONAL VICTIM CENTER

Mr. BEATTY. I would like to begin by thanking Senator Dorgan and members of the Committee for inviting me to testify today about what is obviously a very important issue, the victims of crime. My name is David Beatty. I am Director of Public Affairs for the National Victim Center. Just by way of background, the National Victim Center is a nonprofit organization. It works directly with over 8,000 victim organizations/agencies which provide victim assistance and services to hundreds of thousands of crime victims each year.

Many of these victims and victim organizations benefit directly and indirectly from the VOCA fines. Since the VOCA Fund's creation by the Victims of Crime Act, victims and service organizations have really come to rely on the contributions that are made by the VOCA funds as an essential part of their funding base. In fact, the fund has literally become the lifeblood of the victim's movement.

In fact, I would say that no other Federal legislation that has been passed has probably had a greater impact on the lives of individual victims than the Victims of Crime Act through the VOCA Fund.

I realize that the primary purpose of this hearing today was to discuss issues of collection as it related to the VOCA Fund, talk about what can be accomplished, what remains to be done, and to try to determine what is the best way to accomplish that. But there are other witnesses here today that were much more informed about the specifics of the issue than I am. They were better able to answer the key questions of the day which were who and how.

What I would like to address is the question of why? As we discuss the issue of VOCA funds, I think it is important to remember that the ultimate purpose of fine collection, indeed the ultimate purpose of the VOCA Fund is crime victims. Both exist purely for the benefit of crime victims. And as we discuss and debate these issues and search for a solution to the problem, I hope we never lose sight of the fact that the success or failure of what we do will ultimately be measured by the degree to which they benefit crime victims.

The VOCA Fund itself was really set up for two purposes. I think it is worth mentioning—to provide financial support to individual crime victims through State victim compensation programs and to provide victim assistance directly to service providers through State distribution programs.

In many ways, I think the State compensation programs that are out there have had a greater measurable impact than virtually any other Government-sponsored programs. Violent crime victims are often left not only psychologically traumatized by the crime and physically devastated, but also financially destitute. Medical bills, counseling bills really add up to tens of thousands of dollars. And

---

[1] The prepared statement of Mr. Beatty appears on page 70.

those bills are usually being incurred upon victims at the same time that they are losing their own ability to earn their income as a direct result of their victimization.

Best estimates indicate that there is perhaps $1.5 billion in cost to crime victims every single year. For the majority who do not have private insurance or assets to fall back on, compensation is the only hope that they have and their families have to avoid financial ruin. And apart from these financial implications for the individual victims, they represent the key resource for recovery. I think the President's Task Force on Victims of Crime put it best when it stated: "No amount of money can ease the tragedy and trauma imposed on a victim." However, some financial redress can be an important first step in helping people begin the often lengthy process of recovery. For some, this modest financial assistance can be a lifeline that preserves not only some modicum of stability and dignity, but also life itself.

Compensation really can mean a whole of difference for the quality of life of crime victims. It can make a difference in whether the victim who is living in pain can get the medical assistance that they need to ease their suffering; whether a child who has been victimized will retreat into a world of silent fear and internal turmoil or whether they can get the kind of counseling that they need to facilitate their emotional recovery. Indeed these funds can spell the true difference between financial ruin and economic survival of the victims and their families.

I just want to also point out that not all the costs being paid by victims can be assessed by putting a dollar amount on them. The kind of loss of freedom, the loss sense of security, and of course the loss of a loved one is far beyond compensation. But I think the very least that we can do for crime victims is to help them with the out-of-pocket expenses that they incurred, as a result of their crime. Because after all, they really are the ones who are paying the toll for crime and violence in this country.

But the impact on crime victims really has to go beyond compensation. Victims need more than mere money. They need victim services and assistance. Since its inception, the VOCA Fund has provided absolutely essential services for crime victims in every corner of this country. A thing such as crises intervention, personal advocacy, emergency shelters, transportation, even child care and employer intervention are all absolutely essential for victims in helping them to stabilize their environment so that they can go on with their lives.

There are more than 8,000 organizations who are really the embodiment of the victims movement out there. The vast majority of these organizations are really operating on very limited budget. For many the VOCA money that they receive is not only a welcome source of funding, but it is becoming a crucial source. In that sense it really is, as I said, the lifeblood of the movement. Though the average organization gets a relatively small contribution, $20,000, for agencies operating on a shoestring, VOCA contributions of that amount are really a vital portion of their budgets.

There's been a tremendous amount of growth in compensation in victim assistance programs since it was first created during the last 10 years. VOCA collection have grown from 68 million in 1985 to 21 million in 1992. This year, VOCA will distribute more than $61 million in compensation programs and $65 million in State victim assistance programs. As funding has grown, a number of compensation and victim assistance programs have grown as well. In 1986, there were only 2,000 victim service organizations providing assistance to victims. Since that time, we have seen a 400 percent increase in the services.

Unfortunately, the demand for those services has always outstripped the availability of those services. There simply are not enough resources to go around. But rather than speak in generalities, let me just give you a few examples that have been cited to me by victim service providers and State administrators during just the last week when I spoke with them.

Victims in Alpine, Texas, have to drive more than 200 miles for the most basic victim services which means that a woman who's been beaten by her spouse, has to take 2 days off from work; drive 4 hours to another city; stay overnight; get the counseling they need; drive back that night and all because there is not enough money to provide victim assistance counseling in their immediate area. As a practical matter, victims in Alpine, Texas, do not have victim assistance.

In fact, in Texas, there are only 63 family violence programs that cover 254 counties in the State of Texas. But not surprisingly, many domestic violence victims do not even bother to try to obtain these services. They are left to their own devices and the tender mercies of their abusers. And despite the rising concern over domestic violence in the past few years, this victim population remains substantially underserved. Even today, there are more animal shelters in this country than there are domestic violence shelters.

Typical is the case of the Jefferson County, Domestic Violence Shelter in Arvada, Colorado. In 1993 alone, 524 domestic violence victims were turned away for lack of space; 220 of those were children. Washington State recently funded a program to provide assistance to male victims of sexual assault where usually the most common targets were pedophiles. That program had resources to provide assistance to about 50 clients and within just 3 months, they had over 500 applications for assistance and were absolutely swamped.

I guess the greatest tragedy of this true famine of funding that we are suffering today is that there are thousands of individuals out there who are willing to work for subsistence wages or to volunteer their money full time simply to provide the essential service that victims are literally dying for. And yet we even lack the poultry amount of money that would allow them to set up a program and to sustain the basic services that they want to offer. Every State has to turn down applications for VOCA assistance. Rejection rates in some States run as high as 40 percent.

At the same time, there is not enough money out there to provide existing demand, there is also a growing demand for those services. I think this is partly due to the fact that victims are more aware that the services are available and also because for the first time, with the kinds of programs that are being provided, victims are more willing to come forward and report the crimes and get involved with the process. This growing pressure has placed existing services, increased demands have unfortunately occurred at the same time resources have been declining.

Virtually every program administrator that I have spoken to in the last year can tell the same story, and they simply say that their financial support from every source has been considerably diminished. Many of the private contributors and charitable agencies have either reduced their contribution or withdrawn their support altogether. State funding for victim assistance and compensation is being scaled back as a direct result of budget cuts or as a reduction of the collection of fines that are earmarked for victim services.

And these reductions are unfortunately occurring at the same time that we are seeing a reduction in the collection of VOCA Funds. Fine collection dropped 60 percent from 1992 to 1993 down from $221 million in that year to $144 million, and the possibility remains this year that funding may be down again. This really bowed some very dangerous circumstances for an awful lot of crime victim service organizations that are out there. Many are already curtailing their services due to reduced resources. Others are being forced to divert their precious resources into actually fund-raising to make up the difference, and others are simply closing their door.

Again, an example, Texas has had to reduce the cap of maximum awards for organizations from $50,000 to $40,000. And all of the organizations who are getting the maximum are now scrambling to try to come up with that extra $10,000. This year Texas also has had to defund programs. Defund valuable programs like the court appointed special advocate program which is a program that provides volunteer advocates for child victims of sexual assault and abuse. In many cases, these advocates are the only ones who are there to represent the children, because in many cases the abuser is actually one of the parents.

We have also had to reduce the compensation that is available. Texas has had to reduce to about 40 percent payment on total claims. Where compensation is insufficient, in terms of a statewide fund, they simply had to start creating waiting lists. Some of these waiting lists for compensation funds are over a year long. That is very discouraging because the need for compensation assistance is really immediate to the time of the crime. As one advocate put it, compensation delayed is really compensation denied.

Due to these severe economic downsizing, both from a public and private perspective, victim services are really finding themselves in an ever-increasing reliance on VOCA Funds. The financial crunch is quickly becoming a financial crisis. Organizations are not only losing ground, but there very existence is being threatened. The need for additional Federal assistance is becoming absolutely imperative. I think every possible source of additional revenues should be fully explored. Ways to enhance fees and fines and forfeitures should be carefully examined.

However, none of this is going to be of any use whatsoever unless the debts that are created by these fines and fees are collected. By conservative estimates, we have heard as much as $4 billion today. If you go on the conservative side, estimate that there is $3 billion in outstanding funds. If we could collect just 3 percent of that, that would be the equivalent of $90 million in additional money for

VOCA Funds. That would go far to try to address the really acute crisis that we are dealing with here.

Now as I said earlier, I am not really here to engage in a debate over the criminal debt collection policies for the Federal Government, and I do not tend to be an expert in this issue. But I know one thing something needs to be done and we need to do everything that we can possibly think of to address this issue. I am very concerned that time is slipping by. Each day that we wait for the development of a comprehensive plan is another day precious dollars are literally slipping through the hands of victims. Even as a layman, I know that with each passing week, thousands and thousands of dollars that were collectible are becoming uncollectible. And as this money disappears, the hopes that victims have for their own recovery that could result from those resources are slipping away as well.

The millions of dollars that might have gone to help victims are being specifically designated to courts for collections. Now originally when that slice of the pie was carved up for collections, I think victims felt that it was a good investment. It was an investment that they felt would ultimately provide a greater return. Now I think victim advocates and victim organizations across the country are really beginning to wonder whether that investment was a wise one. A great deal of money has been spent and as we kind of learned today, there are some real questions as to what dividends, if any, we have gotten for that investment.

As the ultimate beneficiaries of the VOCA Fund, I think victims have the right to question the progress of collection efforts today and the right to expect an answer. During this critical time of financial crisis, the entire victims' movement is anxiously awaiting an answer to this collection problem. Anxious because each day money is slipping away. And with it go victims' organizations and victims themselves. For them, the answer has already come too late.

Courses being chartered by those responsible for the Fund will directly affect the health and well being of millions of crime victims. Yet remember that the life prevalency studies indicate that five out of six Americans will fall victim of violent crime during their life times. Virtually everyone in this country has a stake in the debate over what happens with funding of victims' service and a stake in the outcome of these deliberations.

Speaking on behalf of the National Victim Center and as a representative of victim advocates, we urge our elected representatives and appointed representatives to develop a plan that will overcome whatever barriers lay between the recovery of the resources earmarked for the Fund and the distribution of those resources to crime victims. We need to stop the hemorrhaging of the victims' movements lifeblood at its source. A failure to do so will not only debilitate, it could prove fatal to an awful lot of organizations and advocates who have dedicated their lives to repaying this Nation's debt to the citizens it was unable to protect.

I hope that we will not abandon our Nation's crime victims in what is truly the greatest hour of need and I hope we will remember the reason that we are all here today. And above all, I hope that we will remember the crime victim.

Senator DORGAN. Mr. Beatty, thank you very much. The purpose of the hearing was to try to understand what is collectible and what is not and how do we develop a better plan to collect what is owed from criminals. And as you know that collection goes into the Fund that you have been describing. I am going to submit questions to the Justice Department that deal with forfeitures, because forfeitures do not go to that Fund and I am concerned that in some instances they convert to forfeiture what should have been paid in fines and what should really be in the Fund for the victims.

But your contribution is very helpful and I must be over at a meeting in the Senate now, so I am going to have to adjourn the hearing, but we very much appreciate your different perspective and appreciate your submitting the testimony today.

This hearing is adjourned.

[Whereupon, at 12:21 p.m., the Committee adjourned, subject to the call of the Chair.]

APPENDIX

RESTITUTION, FINES, AND FORFEITURE: ISSUES FOR FURTHER REVIEW AND OVERSIGHT

The Senate Committee on Governmental Affairs asked GAO to summarize its work on federal criminal debt collection efforts, emphasizing those areas that could be improved. GAO obtained information on the amount of outstanding criminal debt, the status of the National Fine Center, and the nature and operation of criminal and civil forfeiture laws.

Criminal monetary penalties, consisting primarily of fines and restitution, are important tools in the urinal justice system and serve both punitive and remedial purposes. Most criminal fine payments go to the Crime Victims Fund, which is used for grants to support victim assistance programs. Restitution orders are designed to compensate identifiable victims for financial loss suffered as a result of the defendant's crime.

According to the Justice Department, outstanding criminal debt grew from $0.3 billion to $3.6 billion between fiscal years 1985 and 1993. Much of this increase is attributable to penalties imposed in financial institution fraud cases. Because of severe data limitations and other factors, it is extremely difficult to assess how effectively federal agencies collect criminal debts or how much of the outstanding debt is realistically collectible.

The most important step to enhance debt collection efforts would be for the Administrative Office of the United States Courts to make the National Fine Center (NFC) fully operational. The NFC is intended to centralize criminal debt collection and to develop a comprehensive data base providing current information on the payment of criminal debt imposed by federal courts. Its implementation has been delayed, however. The Administrative Office now is developing a new two-part NFC implementation plan, and expects that the first phase of the NFC will be operational nationwide by September 1, 1996.

While distinct from criminal fines and restitution, asset forfeiture authorities are an important component of law enforcement efforts to deprive criminals of the proceeds and instruments of their crimes. They permit assets to be seized before or even without a criminal conviction, thereby potentially overcoming one limitation on collection of fines and restitution—the diversion of a defendant's assets prior to conviction. Most forfeiture proceeds are used to fund law enforcement activities. According to the Justice Department, there may be opportunities for greater use of forfeiture through such steps as more effective financial investigations. On the other hand, as Justice also recognizes, concerns have been raised about overly aggressive use of forfeiture by law enforcement agencies. Another concern is that forfeiture may reach assets that might otherwise be available for restitution payments to crime victims.

GAO/T–GGD–94–178

PREPARED STATEMENT OF HENRY R. WRAY

Mr. Chairman and Members of the Committee:

We appreciate the opportunity to discuss criminal debt collection efforts of the federal government. With the outstanding criminal debt balance having exceeded $3.6 billion at the end of fiscal year 1993, we believe that the government's systems for imposing, collecting, enforcing, and accounting for criminal debt deserve scrutiny.

At your request, our testimony summarizes GAO's previous work on criminal monetary penalties, emphasizing such areas as: efforts to collect criminal debt arising from financial institution fraud; the status of the National Fine Center; use of the Crime Victims Fund; and the relationship between asset forfeiture and criminal debt collection. We obtained updated information on the amount of outstanding criminal debt, Justice's efforts to improve criminal debt collection efforts, and the status of the federal courts' efforts to automate the accounting and collection system for criminal debt. In addition, we obtained information on the nature and operation of criminal and civil forfeiture laws.

BACKGROUND

Criminal monetary penalties are important tools of the criminal justice system, serving both punitive and remedial purposes. Upon conviction of a criminal defendant, courts may impose one or all of four monetary penalties:

(1) Fines—an amount the court sets as punishment[1] Fines that are not paid in a timely manner may accumulate interest and penalty charges.

(2) Restitution—amounts paid to identifiable crime victims and intended to make them whole.[2]

(3) Special Assessments—fixed amounts, ranging from $25 to $200, assessed for each count upon which the defendant is convicted.[3]

(4) Reimbursement of costs—an amount equal to the court and legal costs of the trial.

In arriving at the sentence, the judge is to consider a number of statutorily imposed factors. When deciding whether to impose a fine, and if so what amount to impose, courts are to consider a defendant's income, earning capacity, financial resources, the burden placed on a defendant, and other factors. If the court decides to order restitution, it also must consider a number of factors, such as the amount of the loss sustained by any victims as a result of the crime and the defendant's ability to pay. In making these sentencing decisions, the court is to consider recommendations made by the U.S. Attorney's office (USAO) and information contained in the presentence investigative report prepared by probation officers. This report includes information on the defendant's financial condition.

Upon determination of sentence, the court is to prepare and issue a Judgment and Commitment Order (J&C) specifying the terms of that sentence. In general, fines and restitution are due immediately unless the sentencing court provides for payment on a specific future date or in installments.[4] If a defendant is ordered to pay special assessments, restitution, and a fine, payments are applied in that order, with restitution taking precedence over fines.[5]

Unlike restitution, which is paid to identifiable victims of particular crimes, special assessments and most fines are to be deposited into the Crime Victims Fund, administered by the Department of Justice's Office for Victims of Crime. The fund is used to support judicial branch criminal debt collection activities (discussed later in this statement) and to make grants to State and local agencies that provide compensation and assistance to crime victims in general.[6] In fiscal year 1993, $144.7 million was deposited into the fund, and $138.5 million was later awarded in grants

---

[1] The Federal Sentencing Guidelines require courts to impose fines in all criminal cases, except where the defendant establishes that he or she is unable to pay and is not likely to become able to pay any fine. In general, the maximum fine permitted by law upon each count of conviction is $250,000 for a felony or any misdemeanor resulting in death. However, higher or lower limits may apply when specified by statute. United States Sentencing Commission, *Guidelines Manual*, § 5E1.2 (Nov. 1993).

[2] The Victim and Witness Protection Act of 1982 (P.L. 97–291) provides the overall framework for federal orders of restitution. Under the act, a district court is empowered to order a convicted defendant to make restitution to any victim of the offense. In the case of a misdemeanor, restitution may be ordered in addition to or in lieu of any other penalty authorized by law. With a felony, restitution must be in addition to some other penalty.

[3] The Victims of Crime Act of 1984 (P.L. 98–473) required courts to impose special assessments against convicted persons. For any offense committed after November 18, 1988, the court an assessment of up to $25 against an individual and up to $125 for an organization convicted of a misdemeanor. For a felony conviction, the court makes an assessment of up to $50 against individuals and up to $200 against organizations. Assessments are imposed to offset the cost of programs authorized under the act.

[4] Installment payments on fines may not exceed 5 years, excluding any period the defendant is imprisoned for the offense.

[5] *Sentencing Guidelines* at § 5E1.1.

[6] The first $6.2 million deposited to the fund in fiscal years 1992 through 1995 and the first $3 million in each subsequent fiscal year is to be available to the judicial branch for administrative costs to carry out its criminal debt collection functions. Additional deposits are to be available for victim compensation and assistance grants in amounts specified by law. Prior to fiscal year 1993, caps were imposed on amounts that could be deposited to the fund, with any excess to be deposited in the general fund of the Treasury. The cap was removed beginning in fiscal year 1993.

for victim services. Figure 1 shows the amounts received and awarded by the fund since fiscal year 1985, along with the fund's cap on deposits.

Figure 1: Crime Victims Fund Cap, Deposits, and Awards

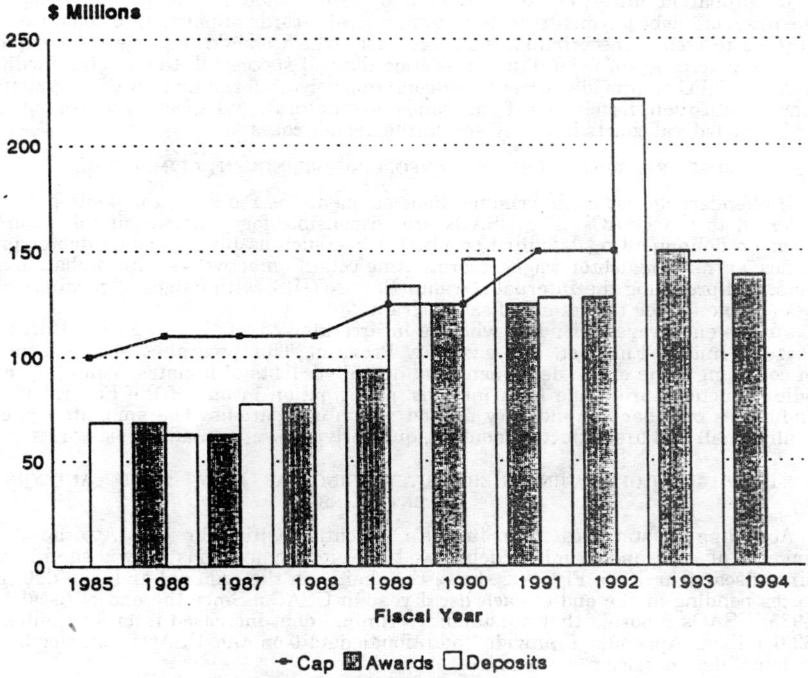

Source: GAO analysis of Administrative Office of the U.S. Courts' data.

CRIMINAL DEBT COLLECTION RESPONSIBILITIES ARE FRAGMENTED

Criminal debtors make payments directly to victims or to the local offices of one of three different agencies: the USAO, probation office, or the Clerk of Court. Presently, the USAOs, Clerk of Courts, and probation offices in the 94 judicial districts have entered into memorandums of understanding which detail the agreed upon division of criminal debt collection duties in each district

According to Justice, this fragmentation of criminal debt collection responsibilities arises partly from changes in the law. Prior to 1985, the Clerks of Courts were responsible for receipt of payments made by defendants on criminal fines and restitution. The Criminal Fine Enforcement Act of 1984[7] made the Attorney General responsible for receiving payments on criminal fines imposed on or after January 1, 1985. The act also provided that for restitution ordered on or after January 1, 1985, offenders could pay restitution directly to victims or to victims through the Attorney General. Later, the Criminal Fine Improvements Act of 1987[8] transferred responsibility for receiving criminal fine and assessment payments from Justice back to the courts. Depending on how the J&C is written, however, courts may order defendants to pay restitution to victims either directly or through one of those sources.

FEDERAL COURTS ARE INITIALLY RESPONSIBLE FOR CRIMINAL DEBT COLLECTIONS AND ACCOUNTING

The Criminal Fine Improvements Act of 1987 addressed the need for a centralized collection system. The act centralized criminal debt collection responsibility within the Administrative Office of the U.S. Courts (AOUSC). Congress contemplated that the director of the AOUSC would establish a single national center within the judi-

[7] P.L. 98–596.
[8] P.L. 100–185.

cial branch for processing fines, restitution, and special assessments. The National Fine Center (NFC) will be the result of this effort.

The NFC is intended to streamline and centralize the criminal debt collection process, providing continuity of federal debt collection data and less duplication of effort. The NFC is to track and collect criminal debts for all 94 judicial districts. Local probation offices, clerks of court, and USAOs should no longer be responsible for receiving debt payments or maintaining local records of payment or balance. The NFC is to create one criminal debt database, which should improve the completeness and accuracy of federal debt collection data. If successful, the database will enable the NFC to provide current and comprehensive information on the payment of fines, restitution, forfeitures of bail bonds or collateral, and special assessments imposed by federal courts in felony and misdemeanor cases.

JUSTICE IS RESPONSIBLE FOR ENFORCING DELINQUENT CRIMINAL DEBT

If offenders do not make criminal debt payments as required, the debts are to be referred to the USAOs. The USAOs are responsible for taking legal collection actions on delinquent or defaulted criminal debts, such as filing liens on debtor properties, garnishing debtor wages, coordinating collection activities with probation officers, and providing the Internal Revenue Service (IRS) with names of criminal debtors eligible for the tax refund offset program.[9]

Justice encourages offenders who are incarcerated to participate in the Bureau of Prisons' Inmate Financial Responsibility Program. This program provides a means of collecting some of the delinquent and defaulted debts of inmates. Voluntary periodic deductions are made from inmates' participation in one of the Federal Prison Industries or other non-industry related prison occupations. The amounts are generally small and are deducted monthly, quarterly, or semiannually from wages.

THE AMOUNT OF CRIMINAL DEBT OUTSTANDING HAS GROWN SIGNIFICANTLY IN RECENT YEARS

According to statistics from Justice's Executive Office for U.S. Attorneys, the amount of civil and criminal debt owed the government has grown significantly since fiscal year 1985. Figure 2 shows the change in the criminal and civil debt balances pending at the end of each fiscal year in USAOs. Since the end of fiscal year 1985, USAOs reported that outstanding criminal debt increased from $0.3 billion to $3.6 billion. Appendix I provides additional detail on the USAOs' total civil and criminal debt caseload and balance.

[9] The IRS Offset Program is another means used to obtain payments on outstanding criminal debt. Once notified by Justice of debtors with outstanding criminal debts, IRS can offset any of the debtors' tax refunds against the amount of criminal debt owed.

Figure 2: Change in USAO Outstanding Criminal and Civil Debt Balances

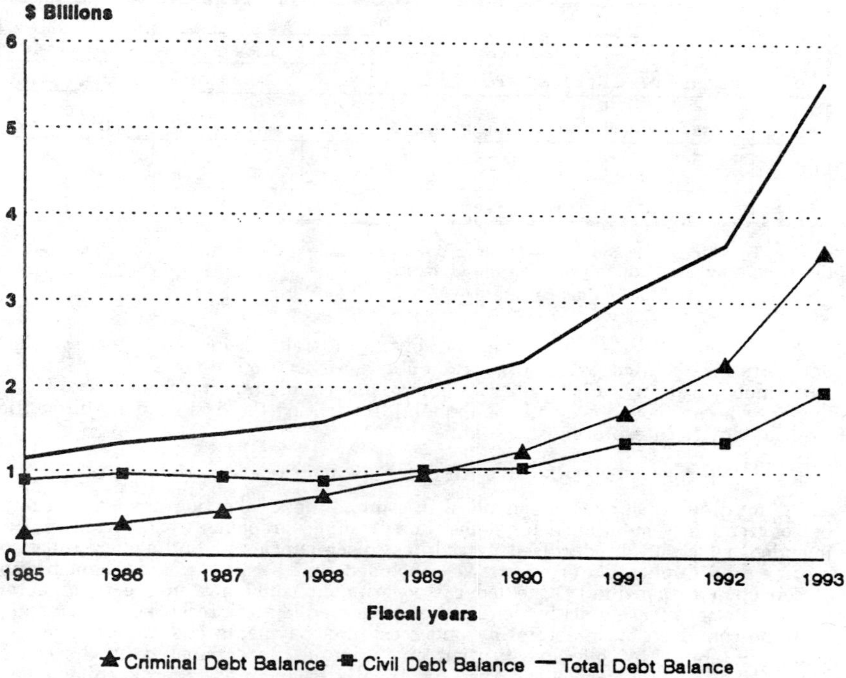

Source: GAO analysis of Justice data.

A large proportion of the outstanding criminal debt is owed by a relatively small number of bank and thrift offenders. According to information from Justice, $1.7 billion (47.4 percent) of the total $3.6 billion criminal debt balance involves as many as 3,576 offenders sentenced in "major"[10] financial institution fraud (FIF) cases.[11] Moreover, according to a Justice official, 88 percent of all the restitution due in FIF cases is owed by only 108 individuals. An analysis of data from cases that Justice determined to represent the 50 largest criminal debts owed to the United States revealed similar findings: Debts associated with individuals convicted of FIF offenses constitute nearly three-quarters of both the criminal debts imposed and criminal balance outstanding from those 50 cases. Table 1 summarizes the results from that analysis, separating those cases that are FIF-related from those that are not.

[10] Justice defines a "major" bank and thrift fraud case as one in which (a) the amount of fraud or loss was $100,000 or more; or (b) the defendant was an officer, director, or owner (including shareholder); or (c) the schemes involved multiple borrowers in the same institution; or (d) the case involved other major factors. We have no information on whether all 3,576 offenders in these "major" fraud cases were sentenced to pay criminal monetary penalties.

[11] According to the U.S. Sentencing Commission's 1992 Annual Report, 12,793 defendants were ordered by federal courts to pay some fine and/or restitution during fiscal year 1992 alone.

Table 1: Summary of the 50 Largest Criminal Debts Owed to the United States

Criminal Debt	Non-FIF (n = 14)		FIF						Total (n = 50)	
			In prison (n = 22)		Not in prison (n = 14)		Subtotal (n = 36)			
	$ millions	Percent	$ millions	Percent	$ millions	Percent	$ millions	Percent	$ millions	Percent
Amount Imposed	213.2	100.0	384.1	100.0	224.6	100.0	608.8	100.0	822.0	100.0
Amount Paid	0.2	0.0	1.0	0.3	2.9	1.3	4.0	0.6	4.1	0.5
Balance	229.3	107.6	383.1	99.7	221.7	98.7	604.8	99.4	834.2	101.5

Note: Totals may not add across or down due to rounding. Additionally, some balances exceed the amount imposed due to penalties and interest.

Source: GAO analysis of Justice data.

Table 1 also illustrates that over half of the FIF-related offenders who owe those debts are incarcerated. With only these data, however, we are not able to determine what amount, if any, of the $221.7 million balance outstanding from those FIF offenders who are not in prison is delinquent, illustrating the first of many difficulties associated with interpreting such data.

NUMEROUS DIFFICULTIES HINDER FEDERAL COLLECTION EFFORTS

The multiplicity of agencies involved in criminal debt collection has led to a number of frequently mentioned problems. For example, problems we reported in 1985 included a lack of standardized procedures, discrepancies among agency collection records, and duplication of effort. We concluded that because of the fragmentation of collection responsibility, the federal government could not ensure that debtors who did not pay were quickly identified and pursued.[12] More recently, Justice stated that the confusion over monitoring and receipting payments has impeded the government's ability to collect restitution and criminal fines imposed by the courts. AOUSC has also acknowledged that historically fragmented recordkeeping among the 94 different judicial districts has created a situation in which systems are usually inconsistent and tend to differ from court to court.

As a result, no one is able to determine with certainty how much is due and how much has been collected. Yet even if that basic accounting data were available, the lack of other critical evaluative information might still preclude an independent review of how effectively or efficiently the government collects criminal debt.

COMPLETE AND RELIABLE DATA ON BALANCES DUE NOT AVAILABLE

At the outset, the federal government lacks complete, reliable data on criminal debt balances. As noted before, AOUSC is initially responsible for accounting for criminal debt. But because the NFC is not yet operational, there is no automated, centralized national data system. Both the courts and Justice maintain some data on outstanding debt, but for a variety of reasons, those data may not agree, thus limiting their quality and usefulness.

For example, neither set of data may record interest or penalties that should be posted to some accounts. According to Justice, because the USAOs have better automated systems, the courts often ask them to record penalties and interest for criminal debt accounts. But in a review of criminal debt collection practices in 10 USAOs in 1993, Justice's Inspector General found that 8 of the 10 USAOs they visited pursued no penalties, and 2 USAOs had waived both interest and penalties for all delinquent debts.

A second major shortcoming of the publicly reported data on criminal debt balances is the lack of critical sentencing information. For example, the systems do not indicate the terms of the fine or restitution orders. As a result, as indicated earlier by Table 1, although the data may suggest the existence of a large outstanding criminal balance, depending upon how the J&C is worded, an offender may owe nothing until the last day of supervised release.

A step in the right direction of clarifying the amount of criminal balances outstanding would be for Justice to reclassify some of the criminal debt that appears uncollectible. This debt could then be deleted from the total balance due. In a recent

[12] *After the Criminal Fine Enforcement Act of 1984—Some Issues Still Need to be Resolved* (GAO/GGD-86-02, Oct. 10, 1985).

report on USAO criminal debt collection efforts, Justice's Inspector General found that 33 percent of all criminal debts outstanding in fiscal year 1991, worth an estimated $565 million, were older than 3 years, and collection rates for those debts were "materially low." To enhance the estimated net realizable value of the open criminal debts, the Inspector General recommended identifying those as uncollectible.[13]

DATA ON AMOUNTS PAID BY OFFENDERS IS INCOMPLETE

Until the NFC is fully operational, the government will continue to lack complete and reliable data on the total amount of criminal debt that federal offenders have paid. This is because courts have ordered offenders to pay restitution to victims through the clerk of court, probation office, USAO, or directly to the federal or nonfederal victim. According to Justice, a high percentage of large FIF cases surveyed had restitution ordered to be paid directly to the victim. Private victims may collect, but there is no mechanism by which those collections are reported to any governmental entity.

Athough the USAO, clerk of court, and probation office in each district have procedures for sharing information on amounts received in their offices, payment data may still disagree. During our earlier review of the National Fine Center,[14] we noted that in the Eastern District of North Carolina, reconciling differing balances for the district's 2,500 accounts took over a year. In addition, Justice's Inspector General noted that because of a variety of problems, USAO data may not accurately reflect criminal debt payments received through the Inmate Financial Responsibility Program.

OTHER IMPORTANT INFORMATION NOT AVAILABLE

Of the balance due, how much is realistically collectible? Any evaluation of federal criminal debt collection efforts should be measured against the total amounts that are collectible.

Justice officials have noted that collection rates vary greatly depending on the nature of the offense. The amounts that are collectible tend to be higher with white-collar crime than with violent personal offenses. However, the Attorney General testified in 1990 that only about 5 to 10 percent of losses in FIF cases may be recovered through civil and criminal proceedings. For a variety of reasons, Justice believed that the money disappeared and that there is little or nothing left to collect or recover at the conclusion of the criminal process when sentencing occurs. Additionally, Justice has said that federal courts tended to base their restitution orders in FIF cases not on an offender's current ability to pay, but on the loss to the victim institution.[15] Consequently, this has created an "inevitable gap" between the amounts ordered and the amounts collected.

Efforts to estimate this "gap" are stymied by poor information. On the one hand, Justice has maintained that the collection rate in FIF cases is not unexpectedly low, because there is "historic agreement" that only a fraction of the total losses would ever be recovered. On the other hand, in a study of 59 major FIF cases, Justice found that its collection rate rose to over 30 percent once it accounted for debt that was legally uncollectible (either because the debt had been stayed pending appeal or was not due until the offender was on probation). Justice also said that "a truly accurate picture" of its collection efforts would require further consideration of the offender's financial condition.

---

[13] According to the *U.S. Attorneys' Manual*, criminal fines, assessments, interest, penalties, and court costs imposed for felony offenses may be placed "in suspense" if a current address is not available for the defendant and the defendant cannot be located after reasonable diligence. This policy allows the USAOs to segregate uncollectible criminal fines and devote greater attention to active cases and those where a likelihood of collection exists. In general, the segregation policy does not apply to restitution, fines over 20 years old (which may be closed), fines imposed for offenses committed on or after November 1, 1987, or fines where the defendant is incarcerated and eligible to participate in the Bureau of Prisons Inmate Financial Responsibility Program.

[14] *NATIONAL FINE CENTER: Expectations High, But Development Behind Schedule* (GAO/GGD–93–95, Aug. 10, 1993.)

[15] Studies of two different sets of FIF cases done by Justice in 1992 found that in 83 percent and 90 percent of the cases, courts set restitution based primarily on the loss to the victim institution. The same studies found that courts rarely ordered restitution based primarily on the defendant's present ability to pay. Justice prosecutors have pursued "loss-based restitution" in other white-collar crimes besides FIF, such as defense contractor fraud and health care fraud.

National Fine Center Is Behind Schedule

The NFC was originally scheduled to be operational nationwide by early 1995. The original project plan provided for a pilot development and testing phase to be implemented in 5 pilot districts by December 1992, followed by a 4-year expansion to all districts. In our prior review of NFC, we reported that, as of December 1992, only one of the five pilot districts had been integrated into NFC operations. Because NFC had missed developmental milestones in several areas, we said that full implementation would probably be delayed.

Since then, AOUSC has acknowledged that the NFC project proved to be much larger, more complex, and more difficult than originally expected. It now regards the attempt to establish the NFC in Raleigh, North Carolina, as a prototype from which it drew important lessons about the practicality of the project's attempts to meet user requirements. AOUSC has obligated $5.7 million of the $19 million made available by Congress from the Crime Victims Fund for the NFC.

AOUSC has reported that the prototype experience provided the basis for reassessing user requirements, leading to a new two-part NFC implementation plan. AOUSC began implementing the first part in April 1994. Its objective is to develop and operate a basic billing, collection, disbursing, and accounting processing center and to convert all 94 district courts to this central system as rapidly as possible. AOUSC expects to have the first court operating on the new system by August 26, 1994, converting 23 additional courts to the system during the first year, and converting all courts to the system by September 1, 1996. According to AOUSC officials, this first part will produce a manual system in which Clerks of Courts, probation offices, and USAOs submit hard copies of criminal debt accounting records (e.g., the J&C, collection receipts) to AOUSC, which will computerize the data on a system in Washington.

During implementation of the first phase, AOUSC expects to procure the "enhanced system," which will meet both the accounting requirements and other management information needs. According to AOUSC officials, this system will be an automated system that more closely resembles what the prototype was attempting at the outset. AOUSC expects that the "enhanced fine center solution" will be in place within 5 years.

Relationship Between Forfeiture and Criminal Debt Collection

One of the areas you asked us to address is the relationship between criminal debt collection and asset forfeiture.

Forfeiture is separate and distinct from criminal fines and restitution. Property can be forfeited administratively,[16] through a civil judicial forfeiture action,[17] or as part of a criminal conviction.[18] Forfeited property is disposed of in accordance with the federal statute which permitted the forfeiture. Most often, forfeited property is disposed of by retaining the property for official use by a federal law enforcement agency, transferring the property to a State or local law enforcement agency which participated directly in the seizure or forfeiture of that property, destroying contraband and other illegal property in accordance with the law, or selling the property.[19]

While we have not done any specific work regarding the interplay between forfeiture and criminal debt collection, we can offer several general observations. One issue that has been raised is whether tension exists between the two because forfeiture might remove assets that would otherwise be available to satisfy criminal fines

---

[16] Federal investigative agencies have authority to administratively forfeit cash and other property valued at $500,000 or less and conveyances (cars, boats, airplanes, etc.) used to transport controlled substances without regard to value. Justice policy requires that forfeitures of real property proceed judicially.

[17] Civil forfeiture proceedings are brought against the property itself. Therefore, the forfeiture action is not contingent on conviction of the property owner. However, in order to qualify for forfeiture property must constitute either the proceeds or instrument of criminal activity. The major civil forfeiture statutes include 18 U.S.C. § 981 (Money Laundering/Financial Institution Fraud), 18 U.S.C. § 1955 (Illegal Gambling), 21 U.S.C. § 881 (Drug Abuse Prevention and Control), and 31 U.S.C § 5317 (Reports on Currency Transactions).

[18] Criminal forfeiture is based upon the jurisdiction the court has over the defendant rather than his or her property. If the defendant is found guilty of the crime charged, then property identified in the indictment can be forfeited incident to the final judgment in the criminal case. The key criminal forfeiture provisions include: 18 U.S.C. § 982 (Money Laundering/Financial Institution Fraud), 18 U.S.C. § 1963 (Racketeer Influenced and Corrupt Organizations (RICO)), and 21 U.S.C. § 853 (Drug Abuse Prevention and Control).

[19] Forfeited cash and proceeds of sale are deposited into the Justice Assets Forfeiture Fund or the Department of Treasury Assets Forfeiture Fund. Deposits to the Justice Forfeiture Fund between fiscal years 1985 and 1993 totaled $3.2 billion. See Appendix II for additional information on how the Justice Asset Forfeiture funds were disbursed.

and restitution orders. This does not appear to be a problem with respect to fines since allowing defendants to pay their fines from forfeiture proceeds would in effect enable them to benefit from their ill-gotten gains.

The effect of forfeiture on restitution is more problematic. For example, assets seized through administrative and civil forfeiture generally are not available for restitution. Therefore, forfeiture may divert assets from restitution and, thus, the crime victims. On the other hand, assets might not have been available for restitution had they not been seized in advance of a conviction.

Forfeiture may complement fines and restitution in the law enforcement arsenal as a means of depriving criminals of the fruits of their crimes. Fines and restitution are imposed only after conviction of a crime. By that time, the defendant may have dissipated or diverted assets. By contrast, forfeiture reaches assets before or even in the absence of a criminal conviction.

Law enforcement officials view asset forfeiture as an effective method to strip away the proceeds and instruments of such criminals as drug traffickers, members of organized crime, and money launderers, and thereby to dismantle their criminal enterprises. In fact, a recent Justice report suggested that there may be opportunities to make greater use of forfeiture through such steps as more effective financial investigations. On the other hand, as the same Justice report recognized, concerns have been raised that asset forfeiture might be used too aggressively by law enforcement agencies.

Issues For Further Review and Oversight

We do not know how much in criminal debt collections should reasonably be expected. While Justice has stated that one should not expect large amounts of collections, it has taken some actions that may improve criminal debt collections. For example, USAOs have implemented a criminal debt management plan that focuses on the identification and active enforcement of collectible criminal debts. Also, the Executive Office for U.S. Attorneys is making numerous efforts to work with the Resolution Trust Corporation and Federal Deposit Insurance Corporation to establish procedures to identify, reconcile, prioritize, and develop collection strategies for FIF debts.

These are positive steps. However, with the total criminal balance growing toward $4 billion, we believe that several areas merit further review and continued oversight. Foremost among those is the NFC. Until the NFC is fully operational on a national basis, efforts to review the government's criminal debt collection performance will continue to be hampered by the lack of fundamental accounting data information on balances due and collected. Considering the difficulties that the AOUSC has experienced in developing the NFC over the past several years and the change in its approach, we believe that continued oversight of the NFC is important.

In our work on bank and thrift fraud, we were often told about the importance of identifying suspects' assets early on during an investigation, before the assets can be moved or dissipated. However, we have little information on how effectively Justice and Treasury conduct investigations to locate assets to be used in collecting criminal debt. Moreover, Justice has acknowledged that efforts to identify assets for forfeiture could be enhanced. Thus, additional attention might be devoted to Justice's efforts to identify and locate assets that could be seized, forfeited, or otherwise used to meet later criminal debt obligations.

That concludes my statement, Mr. Chairman. We would be happy to respond to any questions you or the Committee might have.

APPENDIX I

SUMMARY OF CRIMINAL AND CIVIL DEBT CASELOAD AND BALANCE OUTSTANDING IN THE USAOs, END OF THE FISCAL YEAR

Fiscal year	Criminal		Civil		Total	
	Debt cases	Balance ($000)	Debt cases	Balance ($000)	Debt cases	Balance ($000)
1985	29,219	260,319.6	72,393	887,648.5	101,612	1,147,968.1
1986	44,447	369,228.2	69,441	961,044.5	113,888	1,330,272.7
1987	59,982	515,936.3	57,425	926,117.9	117,407	1,442,054.2
1988	73,057	704,655.8	46,093	883,579.2	119,150	1,588,235.0
1989	84,171	968,487.8	44,039	1,025,133.0	128,210	1,993,620,8
1990	96,455	1,260,382.1	41,366	1,051,678.1	137,821	2,312,060.2
1991	105,649	1,714,470.7	50,355	1,362,885.8	156,004	3,077,356.5
1992	110,898	2,286,911.6	55,727	1,370,952.6	166,625	3,657,864.2
1993	115,352	3,587,400.1	52,290	1,965,382.8	167,642	5,552,782.8

Source: U.S. Attorneys' Statistical Reports, fiscal years 1985–1993.

APPENDIX II

JUSTICE ASSETS FORFEITURE FUND DISBURSEMENTS FISCAL YEARS 1985 THROUGH 1993

Use of funds	Amount ($ millions)	Percent of total
Equitable sharing with state, local, and foreign law enforcement agencies [1]	$1,177.1	36.8
Forfeiture-related expenses	723.9	22.7
Federal investigative and prosecutorial expenses	455.4	14.3
Special forfeiture fund [2]	340.0	10.6
Prisons and jails	427.5	13.4
General Treasury	70.7	2.2
Total	$3,194.6	100.0

[1] Equitable sharing payments reflect the degree of direct participation by state, local, and foreign law enforcement agencies in the law enforcement effort resulting in the forfeiture. This amount does not include $113.2 million in tangible property that was also shared with these law enforcement agencies.

[2] From fiscal years 1990 to 1993, Justice could transfer surplus monies in the Fund, up to $150 million per year, to the Special Forfeiture Fund for implementation of the national drug control strategy.

Note: In fiscal years 1991 through 1993, a total amount of $176 million was declared a surplus available to the Attorney General for law enforcement, prosecution, and correctional activities, and related training requirements of federal agencies in accordance with appropriation acts in recent years. These surplus balanced are available after all expenses are paid and prior year adjustments are made. Of the total surplus amount, $109.4 million has been allocated to various federal agencies as of the end of fiscal year 1993. In fiscal year 1994, the Attorney General has advised Congress of her intention to allocated additional surplus funds in the amount of $65.4 million.

Source: GAO analysis of Justice data.

APPENDIX III

RELATED GAO PRODUCTS

National Fine Center: Expectations High But Development Behind Schedule (GAO/GGD–93–95), August 1993.

Bank and Thrift Criminal Fraud: The Federal Commitment Could Be Broadened (GAO/GGD–93–48), January 1993.

Office of Justice Programs: Discretionary Grants Reauthorization (GAO/GGD–93–23), November 1992.

Victims of Crime Act Grants: Better Reporting Needed for Compensation and Assistance Programs (GAO/GGD–92–2), October 1991.

U.S. Department of Justice: Overview of Civil and Criminal Debt Collection Efforts (GAO/T–GGD–90–62), July 1990.

Oversight Hearings on Asset Forfeiture Programs (GAO/T–GGD–9O–56), July 1990.

Asset Forfeiture Programs: Progress and Problems (GAO/T–GGD–88–41), June 1988.

Asset Forfeiture Programs: Corrective Actions Underway but Additional Improvements Needed (GAO/T–GGD–88–16), March 1988.

Asset Forfeiture Funds: Changes Needed to Enhance Congressional Oversight (GAO/T–GGD–87–27), September 1987.

Justice Department: Impediments Faced in Litigating and Collecting Debts Owed the Government (GAO/GGD–87–7BR), October 1986.

Debt Collection: Billions Are Owed While Collection and Accounting Problems Are Unresolved (GAO/AFMD–86–39), May 1986.

After the Criminal Fine Enforcement Act of 1984—Some Issues Still Need to be Resolved (GAO/GGD–86–02), October 1985.

U.S. SENATE,
Washington, DC, June 28, 1994.

Hon. Byron L. Dorgan, Committee on Governmental Affairs, U.S. Senate, Washington, DC.

DEAR SENATOR DORGAN: I write to offer my support for your efforts on the collection of federal criminal and restitution debt. This is an important component to our national effort to address the issue of crime. Today's hearing is particularly timely as we are on the verge of passing the most comprehensive federal anti-crime legislation ever.

Improving the efficiency and effectiveness of fine and forfeiture collection is essential to our federal efforts to assist victims of crime. The Crime Victims Fund, administered by the Justice Department's Office of Victims of Crime and created by the Victims of Crime Act of 1984, receives over 80 percent of its funding from the collection of criminal fines and other revenues. These funds provide grants to state victims programs and to organizations that assist victims of crime. In 1992, Pennsylvania received over $6 million in federal funding for victims programs. Organizations such as Pittsburgh Action Against Rape, the Womens' Center and Shelter of Greater Pittsburgh, the Anti-Violence Partnership of Philadelphia, the Crime Victims Council of Lehigh Valley, and the Lackawanna County Women's Resource Center received grants from the Crime Victims Fund that enabled them to do their important work. Increasing the collection rate for fines and other revenue will no doubt benefit these groups and the many more like them across the country. In the upcoming weeks I will introduce legislation that will also add to the revenue available to these organizations.

It is clear that those who commit crimes, from petty thieves to financial institutions, must pay their full debt to society. The Congress and the Justice Department must work together to ensure that this is a reality and ensure that those who are the victims of crime receive their just compensation. Your hearings today and your continued efforts to increased the accountability of those who collect this debt deserves our full support. I look forward to working with you in the future on this issue.

Sincerely,

HARRIS, WOFFORD,
Senator, Pennsylvania.

PREPARED STATEMENT OF RICHARD A. AMES

Mr. Chairman and Members of the Committee:

Thank you for the opportunity to appear before you to discuss the National Fine Center. Before I begin, I would like to mention a little about my own background. I joined the Administrative Office this past February. Most of my prior experience was in the private sector, where I spent 6 years as Chief Financial Officer of the Union Pacific Railroad Company, and 22 years with Ford Motor Company in a variety of financial management positions.

I also would like to introduce Nancy Fleetwood, my colleague, who is Chief of our Accounting and Financial Systems Division. Nancy is the new Project Director for the National Fine Center and is in charge of project implementation. Nancy has 15 years of federal government experience, primarily at the Treasury Department, where she successfully implemented several national financial systems and projects.

I would like to start by saying that Nancy and I share your sense of urgency regarding this project. The swift and successful implementation of this project is one of the Administrative Office's highest priorities. The establishment of a system to receive, disburse, monitor, and provide accurate and timely management information on criminal fines and penalties owed to this government and to victims of crime is important to the fair and efficient administration of justice. We are working very hard to make this a reality. I am pleased to be here today to report on the current status of the National Fine Center.

First, an overview:

- *Financial Status:* To date, we have spent $5.7 million of the $19 million authorized by Congress, and we have $13.3 million available to support project implementation.
- *Implementation Plan:* We are committed to having the first court on a national system in two months, 23 courts in the first year (by April 26, 1995) and all 94 courts by September 1, 1996.
- *Fine Collection:* The Judiciary has collected over $560 million in criminal fines since 1990—at the same time we were deeply involved in the planning and development phase of the National Fine Center project.

Now I will review the project status in more detail, beginning with the planning and development phase which was completed April 26, 1994. As I proceed, it will become clear why this phase of the project took so long. Looking back, this project has been much larger, more complex, and much more difficult to implement than originally expected. Simply stated, we tried to accommodate too many system requirements from a broad spectrum of users. We ended up with an initial system design that, based on prototype testing, proved to be overly complex and very difficult to implement. Although we easily could have gone faster and spent considerably more money earlier on a system that probably would not have worked, we chose instead to curtail spending until we were confident we had a system and plan that would work.

PROJECT STATUS

Planning and Development. As background, the Criminal Fine Improvements Act of 1987 transferred from the Department of Justice to the Judiciary the responsibility for receiving criminal fine and assessment payments. In 1990, the Judiciary received funding for the design, development, and operation of a national, automated fine-processing entity that would receive and provide financial information on criminal fines, assessments, and restitution payments. While these accounting functions are located in the Judiciary, responsibility for collecting and enforcing fines remains the responsibility of the Department of Justice.

Accordingly, the Administrative Office began working closely with the Department of Justice, clerks of court, and chief probation officers to build a system that would:

- Meet the Judiciary's statutory requirements for receiving, disbursing, and accounting for criminal debt;
- Replace the disparate financial management systems maintained by clerks of court, probation and pretrial services offices, and U.S. Attorneys with an efficient, centralized system that would meet the administrative needs of all prospective users; and
- Collect, organize, produce, and provide easy access to information on federally-imposed criminal financial sanctions.

Developing a system to accomplish these objectives proved to be significantly more complicated and challenging than initially anticipated. Its complexity is largely due to the nationwide fragmentation of criminal fine record keeping systems. Clerks of court, probation officers, and U.S. Attorneys all track and monitor criminal debt, but they follow different procedures, use different systems, and do not always track all debt elements. Further, these procedures and systems differ from court to court. We found ourselves devoting enormous amounts of time and energy trying to define and design a system that would accommodate the numerous, varied, and often divergent needs and desires of prospective users across the country.

To help clarify this elaborate definition and design effort, we established a prototype fine center in the Eastern District of North Carolina which proved to be extremely valuable in shaping the future course of the project. Prototype testing operations yielded many valuable "lessons learned," including three key conclusions which led us to modify our plans. First, fully accommodating the myriad desires identified by the future users resulted in a "grand design" that would cost too much and take too long to implement. Second, even if we spent the time and money on the "grand design," it might not work. Third, a valuable, efficient system could be developed within a relatively short time period by concentrating on primary user needs, streamlining plans, and refocusing efforts.

The result was development of our current two-step plan, which breaks the National Fine Center project into two phases. Phase I will provide an initial national fine center system with basic billing, receiving, disbursing, accounting, and limited management information functions. This basic system will be implemented relatively quickly and will be enhanced, as we proceed during the next two years, to provide some of the Phase II requirements. Phase II is an enhanced system that will include more comprehensive management information capabilities, along with wide scale, on-line access.

The planning stage for both Phases I and II was completed on April 26, 1994, and we began the implementation stage. At this point, responsibility for the National Fine Center project was reassigned within the Administrative Office from the Office of Court Programs to the Office of Finance and Budget, which is under my direction. I appointed Nancy Fleetwood Project Director. This transition was appropriate because it made the implementation of the National Fine Center project the responsibility of people with functional expertise and experience in implementing and operating accounting systems.

IMPLEMENTATION PLANS

Phase I. We have developed ambitious, but manageable, plans for implementing the Fine Center project. For Phase I, we are focussed on a single goal: To have every court up and running as rapidly as possible on a centralized fine processing system that sends monthly bills to debtors, receives debtors' payments, disburses funds to crime victims and other recipients, maintains accounts, and provides account status. Our timetable is as follows:

- By August 26, 1994, or 120 days after the start of the implementation phase, the first court will be operating on the new system;
- One year later, or by August 26, 1995, 38 courts will be on the national system;
- Another year later, or before September 1, 1996, all 94 courts will be on the national system.

We are now two months into the implementation phase and we have met all of our objectives. To date, we have:

- Evaluated and selected system software;
- Determined hardware, telecommunications, and facility requirements and initiated the necessary procurement actions;
- Identified personnel needs and interviewed candidates; and
- Selected the first six courts to bring on to the national system.

Further, we are:

- Testing and documenting accounting processes and procedures, such as accounts receivable, billing, reporting, and disbursement methods;
- Developing internal control procedures; and
- Finalizing training material and plans for both court and National Fine Center personnel;

We are confident that the activities planned for the next two months will proceed without interruption and that we will meet the August 26, 1994 goal.

Phase II. At the same time that we implement Phase I, we will be developing the Phase II enhanced system. We expect to complete implementation of Phase II within 42–60 months. Meanwhile, the initial system will permit centralized fine center collection and disbursement, and will also meet some of the Phase II management information requirements, while the enhanced solution is being developed.

With completion of the enhanced system, we will have put in place a sophisticated financial center that will greatly improve the federal government's ability to manage criminal debt collection activities. Functions of the system, which are addressed in both phases of the system, include the ability to:

- Centralize receipt of all fines and assessments;
- Compute and assess interest and penalties;
- Send monthly statements to debtors;
- Prepare and mail delinquency and default notices for the Department of Justice, the agency responsible for enforcing debtors' sanctions;
- Provide probation officers, U.S. Attorneys, judicial officers, clerks of court, Bureau of Prisons officials, and others with easy access to account information for individual debtors;
- Make payments to crime victims;
- Provide a repository of national statistical information on criminal debt collection; and
- Produce reports to accommodate the management information needs of the Congress, the Judiciary, the Executive Branch, and other entities.

FINANCIAL STATUS

To date, we have spent $5.7 million of the $19 million appropriated by Congress, and we have $13.3 million available to support project implementation. Of the $5.7 million that has been spent, about 60% was for employee salaries, contractor support, and travel. The balance was for computer equipment, office space, and supplies. These resources were used to develop and install the North Carolina prototype and to redefine needs based on our experiences with the prototype system. The remaining $13.3 million, together with expected future appropriations, will be used to get the 94 courts up and running on the basic system, complete the enhanced Phase II system, and operate the National Fine Center.

Our objective from the start has been to deliver a sound, effective system at the lowest possible cost. In the midst of our original planning efforts, we realized that we could stray from this goal. We found ourselves proceeding along a path that would have required a much greater investment of time and resources than appropriate. Accordingly, we paused to reevaluate our efforts and decided on a new road to follow. I am confident that our current efforts and plans will meet most expectations, and that we will produce a system that reflects careful spending, detailed planning, and sound judgment.

I have attached a letter from Director Mecham responding to recent questions from Senator McCain which I believe will be helpful to the Committee.

I would be happy to answer any questions you may have. Thank you again for the opportunity to appear before you today, and for the support and interest you have shown in this very important project. With your continuing support, we intend to meet our project implementation objectives.

ADMINISTRATIVE OFFICE OF THE
UNITED STATES COURTS

L. RALPH MECHAM
DIRECTOR

CLARENCE A. LEE, JR.
ASSOCIATE DIRECTOR

WASHINGTON, D.C. 20544

June 13, 1994

Honorable John McCain
United States Senate
111 Russell Senate Office Building
Washington, D.C. 20510-0303

Dear Senator McCain:

Thank you for your recent letter requesting a review of the National Fine Center Project. I share your sense of urgency regarding the project. I believe that this letter will provide you with a full report on the issues raised in your correspondence, beginning with a project overview based on your questions:

- *Have we "wasted $19.2 million?"* No. To date, we have spent $5.7 million of the $19 million authorized by Congress, and we have $13.3 million available to support project implementation.

- *Have we lost four years? Are we "starting from scratch?"* No. In fact, the Judiciary has collected over $560 million in fines since 1990. Further, as discussed in more detail later, much has been accomplished during the last four years that positions us to implement an effective National Fine Center.

- *Do we have an implementation plan and timetable for establishing a National Fine Center?* Yes (Attachments I and II). We are committed to having 23 courts on the national system by next April 26, and all 94 courts by September 1, 1996.

In summary, we have completed a very difficult planning phase for a highly complex process involving several government agencies in two branches of government, with initial requirements that proved to be unrealistic. We now are proceeding on an aggressive implementation schedule that will provide a fully operational National Fine Center by September 1, 1996. Looking back, this project has proven to be much larger, more complex and more difficult than originally expected. It has taken longer to reach this stage than we expected, but we easily could have gone faster and spent considerably more money earlier on a system that would not have worked. Instead, we chose to curtail spending until we were confident we had a system and plan that would work.

As background, the Criminal Fine Improvements Act of 1987 transferred responsibility for receiving criminal fine and assessment payments from the Department of Justice to the courts. Funding for the design, development and operations of the Fine Center was first provided in FY 90. The Congress expected the Administrative Office to establish a national, automated fine-processing entity, similar to the successful Central Violations Bureaus, to receive and provide financial information on fine, assessment, and restitution payments. While these accounting functions are located in the Judiciary, responsibility for collecting and enforcing fines remains the responsibility of the Department of Justice.

The Administrative Office has worked closely with representatives of the Department of Justice (including the United States Attorneys) and with clerks of court and chief probation officers to develop plans for an automated system that would: centralize the receipt of all fines and assessments, compute interest and penalties, send monthly statements to debtors, prepare and mail delinquency and default notices for the Department of Justice, make payments to crime victims, generate national statistics, and provide access to account information for probation officers, United States Attorneys and other users.

The project is very complex, largely because record-keeping historically has been fragmented among 94 different districts. Further, separate usually inconsistent record systems and procedures have been maintained by clerks of court, by probation officers, and by United States Attorneys -- and the systems tend to differ from court to court. An enormous amount of effort has been expended so far to define and design a coordinated, comprehensive system that will accommodate the information and administrative needs of all the interested parties across the nation. It is fair to observe that the fragmentation and inconsistency of responsibility complicated efforts to understand and define requirements, and impacted our ability to define a responsive system. Based on the original requirements requested by each user, this system was projected to take five to six years to complete and even this projection was suspect.

A prototype fine center was built in the Eastern District of North Carolina, with the cooperation of the clerk of court, the probation office, and the United States Attorney. It has proven indispensable in drawing the process into focus and in defining the functionality for a national system. It also demonstrated that it would be impractical (cost too much and take too long) to build a system to meet the original "desires"/requirements. This prototype experience provided the basis for reassessing user requirements, which led to our current two-step plan. This plan provides an initial basic fine collection system (described below) that can be completed for all courts by

September 1, 1996 and an enhanced longer-range solution. Prototype operations also provided many other important "lessons learned." For example, we found that the time-consuming and difficult tasks of automating all judgment and commitment orders and of reconciling accounts on old debts among probation, clerk, and United States Attorney offices diverted attention from the goal of implementing a basic fine collection system rapidly.

As a consequence, the Administrative Office, working in partnership with the users, has now completed defining functional requirements for a Phase II enhanced system that will include a major case tracking and management system for all United States Attorney and probation offices, and an initial Phase I basic accounting system that will be limited to accounting requirements but can be implemented relatively quickly and can be expanded, as we go, to provide some of the Phase II management information requirements. The functional requirements for the Phase II enchanced system developed during the planning phase of the project are enclosed (Attachment III). Also enclosed is a recent letter from the Department of Justice outlining how we are coordinating the project implementation effort (Attachment IV).

The current status of the project is as follows:

- Planning: In April 1994, planning was completed on both the Phase I basic fine center system and the longer-range Phase II management system.

- Implementation: On April 26, the implementation phase of the project began. The objective is to develop and operate a basic billing, collection, disbursing, and accounting processing center and to convert all 94 district courts to this central system as rapidly as possible. Specifically, we are committed to having the first court operating on the new system within 120 days (by August 26, 1994) and converting 23 courts to the system within the first year. All 94 courts would be converted within 28 months from project start, i.e., by September 1, 1996. The court conversion timetable is attached (Attachment I) together with the work plan and timetable for the first 120 days (Attachment II). To date, the project is on schedule.

- Enhancements: Concurrent with implementation of the initial, basic system, we are proceeding with a full-scale procurement for the enhanced system, which will meet both accounting and other management information requirements. We expect that the enhanced fine center solution will be in place within 42-60 months. Meanwhile, the initial system will permit centralized Fine Center collection and disbursement, and will also meet some of the management information requirements, while the enhanced solution is being developed.

Honorable John McCain
Page 4

I also wanted to address further your concern that the $19 million appropriated for the project may have been wasted. To date, $5.7 million has been spent for the National Fine Center, and $13.3 million is available to support full project implementation. We have been judicious about the expenditure of funds and can assure you that, as discussed earlier, had we not refocused and refined the overly complicated system contemplated initially to meet everyone's desires rather than their basic needs, we easily could have spent much more on a system that ultimately would not have worked. During FY 90, the first year that funds were available for the Fine Center, operational expenses for collecting fines were charged to the fine center account in error. This error has been corrected for FY 90 and no other operating expenses were charged in FYs 91, 92, 93 and 94. Much of the $5.7 million was spent for development and installation of the prototype fine center in the Eastern District of North Carolina and for subsequent redefinition based on the prototype experience. As discussed previously, many valuable lessons have been learned from the prototype "laboratory," and they have influenced both the planning and implementation phases of the National Fine Center project. Over 60 percent of the money has been spent for personnel salaries, contractor support, and travel. Computer equipment, office space, and supplies account for the balance. The remaining $13.3 million will be used as we convert the 94 courts to the National Fine Center and finish the procurement actions necessary to complete the enhanced system. Privatization is a very real possibility for the enhanced National Fine Center.

You also expressed concern regarding the amount of outstanding federal criminal debt. I should point out that while collection and enforcement of debts owed the Government is a high priority, in fact, some of the debt on paper is simply uncollectible. It results, in part, from the imposition of high fines beyond the normal ability of the defendant to pay, particularly in drug cases. These fines are often imposed to create a lien against all property of the defendant in anticipation that hidden assets might be discovered or the defendant might receive money or property in the future. For example, it is unlikely that the four defendants in the World Trade Center bombing will pay their million dollar fine (see Attachment V). Although the "high fine policy" may result in large book balances of uncollectible fines, the wisdom of the policy was recently highlighted by the actions of one of our probation officers. Through personal and intensive efforts, the probation officer uncovered hidden assets that resulted in the imposition and collection of a $30,000 fine (see Attachment VI for details). We are working with the Department of Justice to answer your questions regarding the amount of the debt and what is being done to manage it better.

Implementation of the National Fine Center will be a major step forward in improving the Federal Government's ability to manage criminal debt. The Center will capture the amount of debt outstanding, collected, and delinquent, and with time, will provide a much better measure of the amounts that can realistically be collected. The

Fine Center also will be a valuable source of information that will enhance the ability of probation officers and United States Attorneys to collect delinquent fines.

In summary, the National Fine Center project is very complex and has been a challenge to define and implement. A workable definition has now been completed, and project implementation is on schedule. Less than one-third of the available funds have been spent to date. We would welcome the opportunity to meet with you or your staff to discuss the project and answer any further questions you may have.

Thank you for your interest and support. If you have further questions or would like to meet to discuss any issues, please call me at (202) 273-3000.

Sincerely,

L. Ralph Mecham
Director

Enclosures

Attachment I

SUMMARY OF COURT CONVERSIONS

TO FINE CENTER

	Number of Courts	
	During Period	Cumulative
• After 4 Months	1	1
• After 8 Months	10	11
• After One Year	12	23
• After 16 Months	15	38
• After 20 Months	20	58
• After Two Years	20	78
• After 28 months	16	94

Attachment II

INTERIM FINE CENTER SYSTEM -- TIMETABLE FOR FIRST 120 DAYS

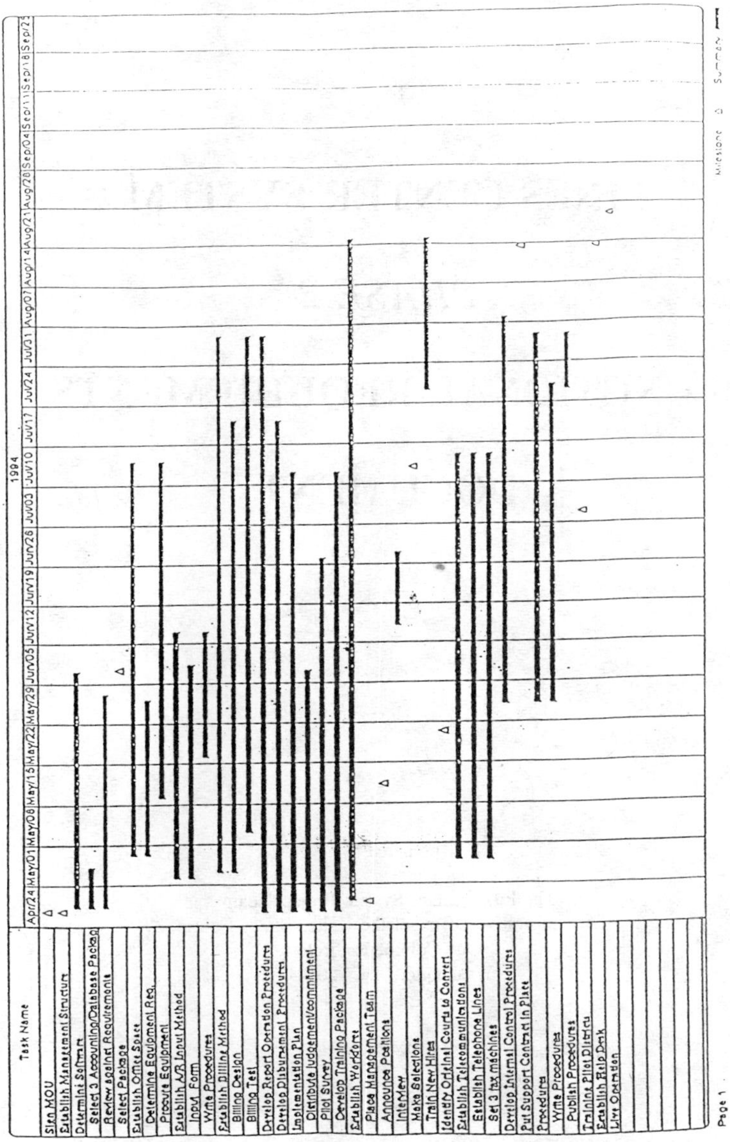

Attachment III
(For Reference)

FINES CENTER SYSTEM

PHASE 2

FUNCTIONAL REQUIREMENTS DOCUMENT

prepared by

The Fines Center System Project Team
Administrative Office of the United States Courts
One Columbus Circle
Washington, DC 20544

February 22, 1994

Attachment IV

U. S. Department of Justice

Office of the Deputy Attorney General

Special Counsel for Financial Institution Fraud

Washington, D.C. 20530

June 6, 1994

Mr. Clarence A. Lee, Jr.
Associate Director
Administrative Office of U.S. Courts
Washington, D.C. 20544

Dear Pete:

I thank you for meeting with us a few weeks ago to review the status of the National Fine Center project. I appreciate the candid manner in which we were able to discuss some of our mutual concerns and accomplishments regarding the Fine Center project. As we discussed, I think it would be good for us to meet on a regular basis, whenever necessary, but at least quarterly to review the progress of the project and to continue our discussions.

The Department of Justice considers the Fine Center project to be of utmost importance. We look forward to continuing our close working relationship with the Administrative Office of U.S. Courts to bring this project to fruition at the earliest possible time.

Since I am in charge of monitoring the progress of the Fine Center Project for the Department of Justice, please feel free to contact me with any questions or concerns you may have regarding Justice's role in the project.

Kristin Tolvstad will continue to serve as DOJ's liaison with the Fine Center under the terms of the present Memorandum of Understanding. We expect that all routine matters between DOJ and the AO will be addressed through Ms. Tolvstad, who will continue to report on a regular basis to me and all interested groups within DOJ, including the Executive Office for United States Attorneys (EOUSA), Justice Management Division (JMD), the Bureau of Prisons, and the other divisions which will be affected by the Fine Center Project. Additionally, we hope to bring in on a temporary assignment a Financial Litigation paralegal to work full time with the project team to add another level of experience to this already well-rounded team.

Ms. Tolvstad will be responsible for coordinating all DOJ-related Fine Center matters with all U.S. Attorney's offices, EOUSA Financial Litigation Staff through Deputy Director Rick Sponseller, and JMD through Bob Ford or Kathleen Haggerty. Mr. Sponseller for EOUSA and Ms. Haggerty for JMD will both serve as members of the Fine Center Working Group.

We eagerly anticipate within the next few months the introduction of the interim Fine Center system into the first courts. As the interim system is being introduced, however, we hope that the AO continues to pursue development of the long-term solution as it was outlined by the Fine Center Working group in the "Phase 2 Functional Requirements Document" dated February 22, 1994. We are committed to supporting the limited, interim system currently under development but it is the long-term solution we are most interested in. At our next meeting I hope we can see and discuss the progress which has been made toward the development of that final system.

Again, I look forward to continuing the good relationship our agencies have had in the past working toward improving criminal debt reporting and collection.

Sincerely,

Gerald M. Stern
Special Counsel for
Financial Institution Fraud

Attachment V

The San Francisco Examiner

May 25, 1994, Wednesday; Fourth Edition

HEADLINE: SENTENCING IN WORLD TRADE CENTER BOMBING

Sentences were handed down Tuesday for the four men convicted in the World Trade Center bombing of 1993. All four were convicted of nine counts, varying from conspiracy to damaging and destroying buildings to explosive destruction of government property, in the bombing, which killed six people. In addition, Ahmad Ajaj was convicted of traveling in foreign commerce with the intent to commit a violent crime, while Mohammad Salameh was convicted of giving false statements in an immigration application.

Mohammad Salameh
A Jordanian citizen of Palestinian descednt; he entered country on tourist visa in 1988, now is an illegal alien.
SENTENCE: 240 years in prison; $250,000 fine.

Nidal Ayyad
A chemical engineer and naturalized U.S. citizen born in Kuwait to Palestinian parents.
SENTENCE: 240 years in prison; $250,000 fine.

Mahmud Abouhalima
An Egyptian native, he had permanent-resident status in the United States and was a former New York cab driver.
SENTENCE: 240 years in prison; $250,000 fine.

Ahmad Ajaj
A Palestinian born in Jerusalem and deported from Israel in 1991.
SENTENCE: 240 years in prison; $250,000 fine.

SEE ALSO MAIN STORY (NO MERCY FOR CONVICTED BOMBERS)

ATTACHMENT VI

PROBATION AND PRETRIAL SERVICES DIVISION
NEWS and VIEWS
A Biweekly Newsletter Published by the
ADMINISTRATIVE OFFICE OF THE UNITED STATES COURTS

WASHINGTON, DC 20544

Vol. XIX, No. 10 May 9, 1994

Johnston Receives Crime Victims Fund Award

by Probation Programs Specialist Kim Whatley

Supervising U.S. Probation Officer James M. Johnston, Jr. (North Carolina Eastern) recently received the Crime Victims Fund Award at a ceremony held on Capitol Hill in Washington, DC, in commemoration of National Victims Rights Week. The award was presented by Attorney General Janet Reno. Chief Probation Officer Dan Martin (North Carolina Eastern) and Probation and Pretrial Services Division Chief Eunice R. Holt Jones attended the ceremony.

Jim was recognized for his outstanding efforts in investigating previously undisclosed assets for deposit into the Fund. During a presentence investigation, Jim found that a defendant had valuable assets in trust, and the court ordered a $30,000 fine. Subsequently, while incarcerated, the offender tried to avoid paying the fine by fraudulently transferring his assets. Working with probation officers in three districts and two United States attorneys' offices through a long court case, Jim successfully recovered the monies. According to the Attorney General, Jim's dedication and coordination efforts are particularly commendable.

The National Forum on Victims Rights is convened each year to allow legislators the opportunity to hear directly from victims and victim advocates about the problems crime victims face in the criminal justice system; to educate the general public about victim rights and services; and to give attendees the chance to meet individually with their own legislators to talk about victim issues. The Crime Victims Fund Award is a high honor, reserved for individuals and groups of individuals whose work for the benefit of crime victims is characterized by exceptional commitment and effectiveness in enhancing contributions to the Crime Victims Fund.

CVF
Award
Jim Johnston

VISION

The Federal Probation and Pretrial Services System strives to exemplify the highest ideals and standards in community corrections.

PREPARED STATEMENT OF GERALD STERN

Mr. Chairman, Senator Dorgan, members of the Committee, I am Gerald M. Stern, the Special Counsel for Financial Institution Fraud for the Department of Justice. The Attorney General has designated me also to oversee the Department's efforts in debt collection. I appreciate this opportunity to provide the Committee with the Department's comments on its debt collection efforts. To the extent that the Committee is also seeking information regarding the National Fine Center, I will comment to the extent I can but must defer to the Administrative Office of the United States Courts for most of the details as that is its mission provided by Congress.

You have identified the purpose of your hearing today by addressing the bottom line—there is $4 billion owed by convicted federal criminals to the United States and to victims of federal crimes. You have correctly stated a fact with which we wholeheartedly agree—effective collection of the criminal debt is a crucial law enforcement mission.

Collection of debt is a task with which the Department of Justice is most familiar. The 93 United States Attorneys in the 94 Federal districts in criminal and civil debt collection recovered 1.63 times the cost of their operating budgets in Fiscal Year 1993. That is 163% of what it cost to run the offices of the United States Attorneys. That is an outstanding accomplishment.

You have noted that the Department of Justice is pursuing and convicting the federal criminals—indeed it is, and successfully so. As of May 31, 1994, we have convicted 4,658 major financial institution fraud defendants and sent 3,197 of them to jail.[1] There is a 96.2 percent conviction rate for all major financial institution fraud cases; a 97.4 percent conviction rate for directors and officers of banks; and a 95.2 percent conviction rate for chief executive officers, chairpersons of the boards and bank presidents.

As the Committee has observed, the Department has been highly successful in obtaining court orders for heavy fines and mammoth restitution orders—in fact, almost half of the present $4 billion total criminal debt inventory—$1.9 billion—was added in Fiscal Year 1993 alone. In major financial institution fraud prosecutions, since October 1, 1988, we have recorded restitution of $1,933,956,000 and fines of $32,792,646 ordered. But you have made another point which we should discuss—that there is *minimal* collection of outstanding debt and restitution orders.

> *Committee Question 1.* Why have there been so many S&L and other Federal Financial Institution related convictions and huge accompanying fines—yet minimal collection of outstanding debt and restitution order.

We believe there has been significant, not minimal, collection of outstanding debt and restitution orders in financial institution fraud cases when all recoveries with respect to the defendants covered by these orders are considered. The Department's efforts to pursue the losses in S&L and other Federal financial institution fraud crimes begin not merely at the time the court orders the defendant to pay restitution or a fine or a special assessment. By that time, a lot of effort has already gone into pursuing lost assets and recovering fraud losses. Our efforts begin at the time the loss is identified and the investigation begins.

In March 1994, the Department collected information on cases in which the FDIC and the RTC were owed restitution of over $1 million. The balance of all restitution orders which had been imposed and were owed to both the RTC and the FDIC was $785,541,243. The amount of all recoveries on restitution orders alone paid on those cases was $25,169,271. The other recoveries, from forfeiture, civil judgments, etc., were $219,066,642. The sum of all recoveries to satisfy these $1 million-dollars-and-over cases' criminal restitution orders was $244,235,913 at that time. When you calculate these successful actions to recover the money lost against the restitution orders, the percentage collected is 31% in the cases which have the largest restitution orders of $1 million and more. The Committee will note that the figure of $244,235,913 in recoveries includes ancillary judgment enforcement actions. Not all of the collection reports are that inclusive of recoveries.

Efforts to pursue assets of the perpetrators of fraud during the investigations, prior to the indictment, and through and after the prosecutions have been vigorous and aggressive. Where there have been assets to pursue and seize and forfeit before, during and after the prosecution, that has been done, not only by the Department but also by counsel from the Federal Deposit Insurance Corporation (FDIC) and the

---

[1] Major financial institution fraud is defined as fraud where the amount of loss was $100,000 or more; or where the defendant was an officer, director, or owner (including shareholder) of the institution; or where the schemes involved multiple borrowers in the same institution; or where the case involved other major factors, in and against the financial services industry.

Resolution Trust Corporation (RTC). Prior to orders of restitution being entered, and even before convictions in a number of instances, the FDIC and the RTC have pursued the losses caused by the perpetrators of the fraud through civil suits and have been highly successful in a number of cases. You will not see those amounts as a decrease in a restitution order, as the money recovered before restitution is ordered is not reflected in the final order for restitution. But it is a recovery against the debt owed to the victims of the fraud. The same is true of forfeiture case recoveries.

For example, over $4 million was recovered prior to sentencing from the sale of one defendant's assets while his codefendant's professional liability insurance policy paid over $61 million to the FDIC on the losses. Still, a restitution order for nearly $13 million remains on which the defendants are paying. The government's quick action, however, resulted in the recovery of some $65 million.[2]

Where a restitution order of nearly $3 million was entered against two defendants, a civil judgment representing more than the restitution order had been entered before conviction of the defendants. $4 million had been collected on the civil judgment. Over $1.4 million of that collection was applied to reduce the restitution order by half.[3] Another civil suit filed by the RTC resulted in a $3.2 million recovery to be applied to restitution of over $5.7 million.[4]

Property involved in the fraudulent schemes has been liquidated to recoup some of the losses. For example, partnership interests in two hotels owned by a subsidiary of a failed victim thrift were sold by the RTC for $111 million.[5]

Forfeiture actions, likewise, have been successful in certain cases, resulting in millions of dollars of asset recoveries. Nearly $11 million in assets from financial accounts, luxury vehicles, vessels, real property, furnishings and other personal property have been recovered and are being liquidated by the Securities and Exchange Commission in a case where there is still a restitution amount of over $40 million.[6] In a $6 million loss, nearly $2 million has been recovered through the forfeiture of real property.[7] In another case, a $751,000 condominium was forfeited to reduce the restitution amount to $1.7 million.[8]

Collection of substantial amounts of the losses represented directly by the restitution orders alone, however, has not been realized. There are a number of reasons inherent to the method of fraud employed by the perpetrators of financial institution fraud which mitigate against the immediate, full recovery of the money lost in such schemes.

In many, if not most, of the financial institution fraud cases where there had been assets not previously recovered by forfeiture and seizure, the assets were squandered throughout the course of the criminal activity. Real estate was falsely overvalued and falsified documents were used to get loans which may never be repaid. Those funds were used in various feeble and ill-fated get-rich-quick schemes which practically guaranteed that there would be no derivative assets to recover. Some of the money gained through fraud was expended in extravagant construction projects or in the pursuit of expensive lifestyles. In one particular case, a defendant has been ordered to make over $14 million in restitution to compensate victims for losses he caused. However, he never received any money in the scheme; thus, there is no reserve of money from which he could readily pay restitution.[9] Unlike some crimes where great amounts of money are illegally made and hoarded, the characteristic nature of these financial crimes was that money flowed freely throughout the schemes and was dissipated in the process.

By statute, the defendant's ability to pay is a factor the courts must consider in determining whether to order restitution or to impose a fine.[10] The sentencing statutes, however, require the courts to consider other factors as well, and place no restriction upon the courts in imposing fines or ordering restitution based on other reasons or other factors the court deems appropriate. In financial institution fraud cases, the government has advocated that defendants be ordered to make restitution to cover the full amount of the loss caused. Consequently, the orders of restitution have been particularly large and ability to pay alone has not been an overriding factor. The fact is that defendants do not appear to have a present ability to make complete restitution on many of the financial institution fraud restitution orders.

---

[2] Louisiana Middle—Howard Kindig, Alton Tullos, Sidney Fazio, 1987–88 FDIC case.
[3] Louisiana Middle—Howard Kindig, and Alton Tullos, 1991–1992 FDIC case.
[4] Kansas—James Cruce, Thomas Dunn, and Thomas Burger, 1991 RTC case.
[5] Central California—Charles Keating, Jr., 1993, RTC case.
[6] Central California—Steven D. Wymer, 1993, FDIC case.
[7] Northern California—Jay Soderling and Leif Soderling, 1987, FDIC case.
[8] Western Washington—Zaki Mansour and Jerome McCuin, 1987, FDIC case.
[9] Illinois Northern—Eugene Cahill, Jr., 1989, FDIC case.
[10] 18 U.S.C. § 3572(a); 18 U.S.C. § 3664(a).

Under federal law, the court is required to consider any impairment the imposition of a fine may have on a defendant's ability to make restitution if so ordered. Specifically, the provision provides that if, as a result of a conviction, the defendant has the obligation to make restitution to a victim of the offense, the court shall impose a fine or other monetary penalty only to the extent that the fine or penalty will not impair the ability of the defendant to make restitution. There have been relatively few fines in financial institution fraud cases and the amount of all fines imposed is small in comparison to the very large restitution amounts imposed. One is compelled to reason that the courts have given due consideration to the reality that a restitution order in the millions and tens-of-millions of dollars will impair the defendant's ability to pay a fine after the payment of restitution.

An order of restitution may be enforced by the United States and by the victim named in the order to receive the restitution. In practice, however, the courts have ordered that defendants pay restitution to victims through a number of sources, including the Clerk of Court, the Probation Office, and the United States Attorney, or that the defendant pay restitution directly to the federal or non-federal victim. This has resulted in complications in both the monitoring of restitution orders and in the receipting and recording of payments made.

While we have computerized all financial institution fraud debt collection information within the Department of which the United States Attorneys are aware, through a monthly hand-reporting system, the lack of an automated, centralized tracking system for restitution and for criminal fines makes it difficult for the government to report with 100 percent accuracy on all restitution and fine payments made. For example, there may have been more money collected in restitution in financial institution fraud cases than has been officially reported by the Department because the Department has insufficient reliable knowledge of what has been paid to private individuals and private banks.

Committee Question 2[a]. What is the current status of the National Fine Center? Please provide an overview of start-up efforts since its creation in 1987.

The Administrative Office of the United States Courts—not the Department of Justice—is charged by Congress with the responsibility to establish an automated criminal debt-processing entity to receive criminal debt payments and to provide current information on the payment and collection of fines and penalties. Once implemented nationwide, the National Fine Center will also include information on the payment of restitution. The National Fine Center should eventually be able to provide the needed information on restitution paid to private individuals and entities.

The Department perceives the urgent need to have the National Fine Center operational nationwide without delay. We have taken great care to see that the courts have maximum cooperation and assistance from the Department. We have coordinated with the AOUSC to resolve policy and programming issues. We have worked with the AOUSC to define the information needs of the components of the criminal justice system. We have participated in outreach efforts. There has been a full-time Assistant United States Attorney working with the courts since last September. Other personnel from the Department have been frequently assisting the courts. There will be a full-time paralegal working with the courts in addition to a full-time Assistant United States Attorney in July. If the courts ask for more help, the Department will make diligent efforts to see that such help is available. The recordkeeping functions and the persistent and determined pursuit of collections by the courts are extremely important tasks which are absolutely fundamental to our efforts to recover criminal debts and to be informed about the recovery of criminal debts in all criminal cases.

In financial institution fraud cases where the amounts owed are larger than they are in virtually any other group of criminal fraud cases, the need for detailed and reliable information from one source rather than the multiple sources from which information presently is derived is critical to coordination of the collection efforts. Information on civil recoveries of judgments against the defendant debtors by private parties and third parties would be extremely helpful as these amounts can be used to offset amounts owed in restitution on the same debts. Through a comprehensive nationwide system of records, information concerning collections in financial institution fraud debts will be greatly enhanced.

Committee Question 2[b]. What is the total outstanding financial institution criminal debt, i.e., fines and restitution? What are the total amounts collected on these obligations?

The total number of fines in cases involving major financial institution fraud through a continuing calculation from October 1, 1988, to May 31, 1994, was 778, for a total amount of $32,792,646. As of May 31, 1994, $3,284,708 of this total had been collected. That is 10 percent of the total imposed, yet the government has 20 years during which to collect these fines and interest and penalties are added to those fines when they go uncollected or are in default. A high percentage of those defendants are either in jail or have recently completed periods of incarceration. Collecting these fines is an ongoing endeavor and we intend to continue to pursue collection aggressively. The money has not been lost.

During the period from October 1, 1988, through May 31, 1994, we recorded 2,249 restitution debts ordered in major cases. Those orders provide for restitution to the federal government, as well as to private banks, individuals or entities.

There has been $34,550,836 collected in major savings and loan restitution cases (both federal and non-federal); $14,365,102 in bank restitution cases; and $361,237 in credit union restitution cases during the period October 1, 1988 through May 31, 1994. These numbers reflect information provided by the United States Attorneys and the FDIC and RTC. As we have noted, there may have been more money than this collected by private individuals and entities who have no duty to report their collections to us. These figures represent a total collection amount of $49,307,175. When other recoveries resulting from execution against defendants' property, from forfeitures and from civil judgments are added to the collection numbers, the collection total becomes $185,263,888 in the major fraud cases alone.[11] That amounts to a 9% recovery of the present *total* outstanding restitution inventory for *major* cases. And one must bear in mind that $900,416,985 of the present inventory was just ordered since October 1, 1992. That is, 46% of the present criminal restitution debt inventory in financial institution fraud cases is relatively recent restitution debt.

108 criminal restitution debts of over $1 million each owed to the federal government accounts for $785,541,243 of the criminal restitution inventory in financial institution fraud cases. Those debts are owed by just 125 individuals.

At the end of February 1994, the top ten debtors who owe restitution to the FDIC and the RTC owed $415,278,720. This accounts for 54% of the restitution owed to the FDIC and RTC. Stated another way, more than half of the total restitution payable to the FDIC and RTC imposed in orders for $1 million and more is owed by just ten people.

Committee Question 3. Is the Victims Compensation Fund adequately capitalized? What percentage of the fund is used to fund overhead and administrative costs?

The Crime Victims Fund (Fund) is not adequately capitalized and no amount at all goes to fund overhead or administrative costs.

The Fund's deposits fluctuate widely each year. This fluctuation has an impact upon the funding available for the various activities and initiatives supported by the Fund. Generally, Health and Human Services receives 6 percent of the Fund for Children Justice and Assistance Act grants and the Administrative Office of the United States Courts receives 4 percent of the Fund.

The Office for Victims of Crime (OVC) administers the remaining funds as follows: 3 percent is used for services to victims of federal crimes and for training and technical assistance to victim service providers throughout the nation and 87 percent is used to supplement state and local services to violent crime victims through Victims of Crime Act (VOCA) state and victim compensation and state victim assistance grants. These two state grant initiatives are extremely important sources of support for violent crime victims throughout the nation.

Participating state victim compensation programs receive a VOCA grant based upon a formula of 40 percent of the amount of compensation paid by the state during the previous federal fiscal year. This assumes that the amount available for compensation grants is sufficient to cover 40 percent of state payouts for compensation.

The VOCA compensation grant funds can only be used for payments to crime victims for out-of-pocket costs that are directly related to the crime. Currently, the ever-increasing scarcity of funding is the most difficult issue facing state compensation programs. A recent survey conducted by the National Association of Crime Victim Compensation Boards showed that 35 state compensation programs are experiencing a financial crisis. Accordingly, these states may delay payment of victim compensation claims, may pay only a percentage of the compensation claim, and/or may temporarily cease to pay compensation claims for certain types of expenses.

[11] The Committee will recall that the definition for a "major" S&L case is not the same as that of a case where $1 million or more was ordered to be paid in restitution. The Committee will also note that the $185,263,888 figure is the one gained from the monthly reporting by the United States Attorneys offices and is smaller than the $244,235,913 recovery figure above because it does not include those recoveries from the sales of property in ancillary judgment enforcement actions, among other calculations. Please note that the two numbers represent a different time period and different reporting criteria.

All states, the District of Columbia, and the U.S. Territories receive VOCA victim assistance grants. Grants are based upon a formula, which gives all grantees a minimum of $200,000 with the remaining amount available for VOCA victim assistance grants being distributed by population.

VOCA grant dollars are used only for direct services to crime victims. Neither the state nor the local victim service provider may use any portion of the VOCA grant funds for administrative or overhead purposes. Thus, grants are awarded to states which subgrant the VOCA funds to local victim service providers who provide direct services. Local victim service providers offer services such as counseling, crisis intervention, emergency shelter, criminal justice advocacy, information and referral, and other services.

State victim assistance programs alone cannot meet the needs of crime victims; therefore, they must make critical decisions on how best to maximize the limited VOCA grant funds. For example, the state of Wyoming's $298,000 1994 VOCA grant is distributed to selected victim service providers, with a maximum subgrant of $6,000. Other states fund only a portion of a crisis counselor's or victim advocate's salary, select for funding only a percentage of the applications received, limit funding to selected types of services and activities, and/or make funding decisions on the maximum number of victims to be served.

Committee Question 4. How does law enforcement utilization of the Seized and Forfeiture Statutes affect a convicted felon's ability to pay court ordered fines and/or restitution?

In summary, federal forfeitures virtually never affect restitution and seldom affect fines. Seized and forfeited property is not available to convicted defendants for the payment of fines. Nor is forfeited property available to convicted defendants for the payment of restitution orders imposed by the courts pursuant to Title 18, United States Code, sections 3663 and 3664. Property that is forfeited becomes the property of the United States and is disposed of in accordance with the forfeiture laws. The policy of the Department of Justice has long been that restitution to victims has priority over the Department's Forfeiture Fund in terms of the disposition of forfeiture proceeds. In every case in which we have statutory authority to do so, we use forfeited funds to pay restitution to victims.

The advantage of forfeiture is that the government is able to freeze assets before the criminal can hide or dissipate them with the result that our collection rate is 100% where the assets have been secured in advance of the forfeiture action. Thus, seizures and forfeitures are used effectively to assist in achieving victim restitution by preserving property before conviction and making it available for restoration or restitution to victims by the Attorney General pursuant to provisions in the forfeiture laws that govern the disposition of forfeited property. By contrast, fines and restitution orders are imposed after indictment, after trial, and after the court has had the time to obtain a pre-sentencing report. By that time, criminals have had ample opportunity to secrete or consume any assets with the result that most restitution orders and criminal fines are uncollectible. Where restitution is concerned, the victim who loses money in a scheme which triggers a federal forfeiture stands a better chance to recover some of the loss, as forfeiture is much more likely than restitution to result in restoration of some part of the victim's losses.

Under all the forfeiture laws enforced and administered by the Department of Justice, the Attorney General has authority to grant petitions for remission or mitigation of forfeitures to so-called "owner victims" who can trace their losses to specific forfeited property. Additionally, some forfeiture statutes explicitly provide authority for the Attorney General to restore forfeited property to victims of the offense underlying the forfeiture regardless of their traceable ownership interest in the property forfeited. For example, with respect to property ordered forfeited under the criminal forfeiture statutes, the Attorney General is authorized to:

> grant petitions for remission or mitigation of forfeiture, restore forfeited property to victims of a violation of [the applicable chapter or subchapter], or take any other action to protect the rights of innocent persons which is in the interest of justice and which is not inconsistent with the provisions of [the applicable chapter or section]; (see, for example, 18 U.S.C. § 982(b)(1) (money laundering and financial institution fraud)).

Similarly, in civil forfeitures of the proceeds of financial institution frauds, Title 18, United States Code, section 981(e)(6) provides broad authority to the Attorney General for restoration of the forfeited proceeds to "any victim" of such fraud. Sections 981(e)(3) and (7) provide specific authority for the Attorney General to transfer forfeited financial institution fraud proceeds to any federal financial institution regulatory agency to reimburse the agency for payments to claimants and creditors of a financial institution, to reimburse the agency's insurance fund for losses, or to restore the agency's direct losses. Transfers by the Attorney General of forfeited financial institution fraud proceeds to defrauded financial institutions as restitution is provided for specifically in section 981(e)(4).

With respect to criminal fines, forfeiture may, in rare instances, compete with fines. In this regard, criminal fines are imposed based upon the statutory fine limits and the sentencing judge's opinion as to the criminal's ability to pay. Forfeitures, by contrast, are limited by law to the profits and proceeds that we can establish by evidence are the gains of the criminal offense and, in some instances, include property used to facilitate the criminal offense. It is rare that the government can put on evidence establishing the forfeitability of all of a defendant's assets.

Assuming that a drug trafficker generates profits of millions of dollars and the government is able to locate, seize, and forfeit a bank account containing $1 million, then that $1 million is not available for the payment of a criminal fine. The sentencing court is normally aware that the $1 million bank account does not belong to the criminal and assesses an amount of fine that takes this into account. However, any other assets of the criminal, even those not tainted by criminal activity, are available to pay a criminal fine.

In this hypothetical, it would be a boon to the defendant to have the government use the forfeiture proceeds that belong to the government pursuant to the forfeiture action to pay off the criminal defendant's criminal fine. Pursuant to federal law, the proceeds of a criminal enterprise do not belong to the criminal. To the extent the government can prove its case, the fruits of the criminal activity belong either to the victims of the criminal scheme or to the government in trust for the public at large. Further, the purpose of a criminal fine is to punish the criminal, a purpose that can be achieved by removing the criminal's own assets. To use forfeited assets to pay off criminal fines would confer an economic benefit on the criminal at the expense of the public.

CONCLUSION

In conclusion, Mr. Chairman, Senator Dorgan and members of the Committee, regarding your inquiry into the development of the National Fine Center, I affirm that the Department has a vital interest in seeing the Administrative Office of the United States Courts achieve the realization of the task that Congress imposed upon it in 1987—to build and maintain a National Fine Center. While the Department is not the entity charged with the task, it has and continues to stand ready to provide whatever assistance the courts require. As for collection of the financial institution fraud criminal debt, please be assured that the Department is committed to continuing its aggressive and determined efforts.

PREPARED STATEMENT OF DAVID BEATTY

I would like to thank Senator Dorgan the Chairmen and the other members of the Committee for inviting me here to address the issue of Federal funding for crime victims.

My name is David Beatty. I am the Director of Public Affairs for the National Victim Center.

The National Victim Center is a non-profit organization which works directly with more than 8,000 victim organizations and agencies which provide assistance and services to hundreds of thousands of violent crime victims each year.

Many of these victims and victim organizations benefit directly or indirectly from Federal VOCA Funding.

Since the creation of the VOCA Fund in 1984 by the Victims of Crime Act, victims and service organizations and agencies have come to rely on contributions from the VOCA Fund as an essential part of their funding base.

The Fund has literally become the lifeblood of the victims' movement. No other Federal legislation has had as great an impact on the lives of our nations' crime victims than the Victims of Crime Act, through the VOCA Fund.

THE VOCA FUND

The VOCA Fund was rather simple in both its conception and its proposed operation.

The authorizing Act provided that Federal fines and appearance bond forfeitures owed by offenders be allocated to the Victims of Crime Fund. In addition, the Act established a special penalty assessment for individuals and corporations convicted of Federal offenses which were also to be paid into the Fund.

Federal courts, prison system officials, and U.S. Attorneys were given the primai responsibility for collection of not only fines, fees and assessments, but also for co lection and distribution of court-ordered restitution.

Once deposited in the Fund, the Office for Victim Assistance was empowered t distribute these monies to the states in the form of formula/block grants. Thes block grants were generally designated for two specific purposes:

1. To provide financial support to individual crime victims through state victi compensation programs; and
2. To provide financial assistance to direct victim service providers (or sul grantees) through state distribution programs.

IMPACT OF THE FEDERAL VICTIM COMPENSATION PROGRAM

In many ways, the state crime victim compensation programs supported by tl Fund have a greater measurable impact on individual victims than any other go ernment-sponsored program.

Violent crime leaves most victims not only psychologically traumatized and phy ically devastated, but also financially destitute. Medical and counseling bills, ofte amounting to tens of thousands of dollars, are incurred by victims while they a simultaneously experiencing a loss of income due to their absence from work as direct result of their victimization.

In 1989, the estimated cost of violent crime to victims was $1.5 billion. Interes ingly, this is also the approximate amount of money currently owed to the Fund b offenders as estimated by the Department of Justice.

For the majority of victims who do not have private insurance or assets to fa back on, compensation may be the only hope they and their families have of avoi ing financial ruin.

Apart from their implications for victims' financial conditions, such resources a often essential for victims' physical and psychological recovery. As stated by th President's Task Force on Victims of Crime:

> . . . No amount of money can erase the tragedy and trauma imposed on [victims]; however, some financial redress can be an important first step in helping people begin the often lengthy process of recovery. For some, this modest financial assistance can be the lifeline that preserves not only some modicum of stability and dignity but also life itself. . . .

Compensation can mean a world of difference in the quality of life for victim struggling to recover from their victimization.

In many cases, it may mean the difference between the victim living in pain c receiving the medical treatment necessary to relieve their affliction.

It could be the difference between allowing a child victim to retreat into a worl of silent fear and internal turmoil, ravaged by self-blame and loathing, or being a forded the counseling necessary to facilitate their emotional and psychological reco ery.

It could also determine whether or not a victim receives the physical therapy the need to allow them to return to work and support themselves and their family.

Indeed, these funds can mean the difference between financial ruin and economi survival for many of the victims fortunate enough to receive this assistance.

Of course, the real cost to victims cannot be measured in dollars. The loss of free dom, the loss of a sense of safety and security, and the loss of a loved one are be yond compensation.

Compensating victims for their out-of-pocket expenses that flow from the crim committed against them seems like the least we can do for those whom societ failed to protect from violence.

PACT OF THE FEDERAL VICTIM ASSISTANCE PROGRAM

Yet crime victims need more than mere money—they need assistance and serv ices. Since the 1970s, victim assistance organizations and entities throughout the na tion have provided support and assistance to crime victims, including crisis inte vention, counseling, emergency financial assistance, personal advocacy, emergenc shelter, transportation, child care, employer intervention, and information about th criminal justice process.

These support services are critical to a victim's psychological well-being and thei ability to stabilize their life and resume normal tasks. They have proven to be th key in gaining the victim's willingness to cooperate with criminal justice official while helping the victim to satisfy their own sense of justice.

For the most part, the more than 8,000 organizations who provide these essentia services, *are* the victims' movement. Yet the vast majority of organizations providin these critical services operate on very limited budgets. For many, VOCA money has become more than a welcomed source of funding—it has become a crucial source.

In that sense, VOCA Funds have become the lifeblood of the victims' movement. Though the average grant to such organizations is relatively small (averaging less than $20,000), for agencies operating on a shoestring, VOCA contributions represent a vital portion of their budgets. State funding and private donations comprise the remaining portion of their funding base.

Together, these organizations and agencies serve millions of crime victims each year representing every category of victimization from child abuse and domestic violence to sexual assaults and drunk-driving, from simple assaults to homicides.

In many cases, victim advocates in prosecutors' offices represent the only link victims have with the criminal justice process and are the only officials in the criminal justice system dedicated to protecting their interests and addressing their concerns as crime victims. Many of these advocacy programs are direct beneficiaries of VOCA Funds.

GROWTH OF VOCA FUNDING AND THE DEMAND FOR ASSISTANCE

Funding for victim compensation and victim assistance programs have increased dramatically during the last ten years.

VOCA Fund collections alone have grown from $68 million in 1985 to a high of $221 million in 1992.

This year VOCA will distribute almost $61 million to state victim compensation programs and $65 million to states for victim assistance programs.

As funding has grown, so have victim compensation and victim assistance programs.

In 1986, approximately 2,000 service organizations existed to provide victims with assistance and advocacy. We have witnessed a 400% increase in that number over the last eight years.

Yet despite the increase in availability of these services, the demand has always outstripped the supply by a considerable margin. There simply are not enough resources to go around.

There are not enough advocates to keep all victims informed about developments in their respective cases, not even for victim notification whenever the offender is released or escapes.

There is not enough money to pay all the legitimate compensation claims made by crime victims, leaving many with no alternative but to file for bankruptcy.

There are not enough beds in domestic violence shelters to provide all spouse abuse victims and their children the opportunity to escape the violence and terror that rules their lives.

There are sexual assault victims who are sitting on nine-month long waiting lists for counseling to help them put their shattered lives back together.

In other words, while the resources (including VOCA Funds) have risen, they are not meeting all the needs of crime victims and, in some cases, are meeting none of their needs.

But rather than speaking in generalities, let me provide some specific examples cited to me by State Administrators and victim service organizations with whom I spoke just last week.

Victims in Alpine, Texas have to drive more than 200 miles for the most basic victim assistance. This means a woman who has been beaten by her spouse has to take two days off from work in order to drive four hours to another city, then stay overnight and drive back, simply because there is not enough money to fund a victim assistance unit in her area. As a practical matter, victim services do not exist for these victims in Alpine, Texas.

In fact, Texas has only 63 family violence programs which attempt to cover victims in 254 counties. Not surprisingly, many domestic violence victims are simply left to their own devices and the less than "tender mercies" of their abusers.

Despite the rising concern over the crime of domestic violence, its victims remain substantially underserved. Even today, there are more animal shelters in the United States than there are domestic violence shelters.

Typical is the case of the Jefferson County Domestic Violence Shelter in Arvada, Colorado. In 1993 alone, 524 domestic violence victims were turned away for lack of space, including 222 children.

Washington State recently funded a program to provide assistance to male victims of sexual assault (young males being the most common target of pedophiles). The program had resources to serve about 50 clients. Within three months, it had received applications from more than 500 victims.

Perhaps the greatest tragedy of this famine of funding is that even though there are thousands of individuals willing to work at subsistence salaries or to volunteer full-time in order to provide the services and assistance crime victims are literally dying for, these individuals lack the paltry funding necessary to initiate and sustain even the most basic programs offering such services.

Every state is forced to reject applications from prospective service providers for VOCA assistance. Rejections run as high as 40% of all applications in some states.

State program administrators have indicated that such rejection rates have had a chilling effect on organizations. Many organizations have simply given up applying for such funds after being repeatedly rejected due to insufficient funds, despite the pressing need for the services they provided to crime victims.

GROWING NEED DURING THE ECONOMIC SQUEEZE

The demand for victim assistance and services has grown dramatically in recent years. This is due in part to a greater awareness among victims of their availability and in part to the greater willingness of victims to report crimes to authorities. The growing pressure placed on existing services by this increased demand is occurring just as available resources for such services are declining.

Virtually every program administrator and service provider to whom we have spoken in the last year indicated that financial support from every source has diminished considerably.

Many private contributors and charitable agencies are being forced by their own dwindling funds to either reduce their contribution or withdraw their support altogether.

State funding for both victim assistance and victim compensation are being scaled down as a direct result of budget cuts or reductions in the collection of fines and fees earmarked for victim services.

This is occurring at a time when VOCA Fund collections are down. Fine collections dropped 60% from 1992 to 1993, from $221 million to $144 million. Total collections for the Fund could drop again this year.

Bearing in mind the fact that many organizations operate on marginal budgets, the reduction in funding could harbor disastrous repercussions for their operation and outlook. Many are already being forced to curtail services, others are being forced to divert scarce resources away from victim services to fundraising, and some are simply being forced to close their doors.

Texas, for example, has had to reduce their cap on maximum awards to organizations from $50 thousand to $40 thousand. Many organizations are scrambling to make up the difference or to reduce services.

This year Texas has been forced to de-fund some programs like the Court-Appointed Special Advocates Program that provides child victims of abuse and sexual assault with a volunteer advocate to protect their rights and represent their interests before the court. In many cases, particularly when the offender is a parent, CASA volunteers are the only people in the system who are able to perform such services. Without them, children will be left to fend for themselves in a system they cannot comprehend, surrounded by adults making demands which they are unable, or too frightened, to accommodate.

Victim compensation programs have been hard hit as well. Texas has reduced its maximum percentage payable for each request to 40% of the total claim as the result of budget cutbacks and reduced Federal contributions. Victims are simply forced to absorb the remaining 60% of their crime-related expenses.

Numerous states, where the victim compensation fund is insufficient to cover compensation claims, have simply created waiting lists. Some victims are forced to wait a year or more before they receive their first check, despite the fact that the need for financial assistance is most acute in the first few weeks following their victimization. When compensation for medical assistance and counseling is delivered years after the fact, it arrives too late to have any real impact. As one advocate put it, "Compensation delayed is compensation denied."

In Maryland, administrators are considering lowering the maximum compensation award, creating maximums for specific categories of compensable expenses, and eliminating some categories altogether as the result of the reduction in Federal funding.

Due to the severe economic downsizing in both their public and private funding bases, victim service agencies find themselves in the position of ever-increasing reliance on VOCA Funds.

The financial crunch is quickly becoming a financial crisis for almost all victim service organizations. Organizations are not only losing ground due to the crisis, but many are threatened with extinction.

The need for additional Federal assistance is becoming absolutely imperative if victim services are to survive. Every possible source of additional revenues should be fully explored. Ways to enhance fines, fees and forfeitures as a funding source should be carefully examined. However, increasing the amount owed by offending individuals and entities will have no effect unless these debts are actually collected.

By conservative estimates, there was more than $1.6 billion in criminal debt outstanding as of 1992. Some have estimated that the number may be closer to $3 billion. If even 3% of that amount could be secured by additional collection efforts, the resulting $90 million would go far to ease the current financial crisis.

Fine Collections

I am not here to engage in a debate over the criminal debt collection policies and programs of Federal Government. I do not pretend to be an expert on the issue of fine collection. I do not know what has been done, or even what can be done, to increase fine collections.

But as an outsider and a victim advocate, I am very concerned that everything that *can* be done to increase collections *should* be done—and done as soon as possible.

I am concerned that each day we wait to develop and implement a comprehensive plan is another day precious dollars are slipping through victims' hands. Even as a layman, I know that with each passing week thousands of dollars in collectible fines become uncollectible. Money that could help victims piece their lives back together is disappearing and with it go the hopes of thousands of victims' seeking recovery.

Millions of dollars that might have otherwise gone to help victims have been designated to improve collections. In fact, an amendment was passed last year which earmarks the first $6.2 million in VOCA Fund deposits to the Federal courts for purposes of collection. When the designation from the VOCA Fund for purposes of collections was originally contemplated, members of the victims' movement felt it was a good investment—an investment that would eventually ensure a greater return. Now victim advocates are not so sure they made a wise investment. A great deal of money has been spent, but no one seems to be certain of what dividends, if any, they have received in return.

As the ultimate beneficiaries of the VOCA Fund, victims have the right to ask these questions and to expect an answer.

During this critical time of financial crisis, the entire victims' movement is anxiously awaiting an answer—anxious because as each day passes, money—and consequently organizations and then the victims they serve—are slipping away. For them, the answer is already too late.

The course charted by those responsible for the Fund will directly affect the health and well-being of millions of Americans who have been, or will become, the victims of violent crime.

In fact, lifetime prevalence studies indicate that five out of six Americans will fall victim to violent crime during their lives. At that rate, it is clear that almost all of us have a direct stake in debate over funding for victim services and a stake in the outcome of these deliberations.

Speaking on behalf of the National Victim Center, and as a representative for victims and victim advocates everywhere, we urge our elected and appointed representatives to develop a plan that will overcome the barriers that lay between the recovery of resources earmarked for the Fund and the distribution of those resources for the recovery of crime victims.

We need to ensure that offenders pay their debt not only to society but also to the victims of their crimes. We need to grasp every dollar within our reach. We need to stop the hemorrhaging of the movement's lifeblood at the source. Failure to do so will prove debilitating, if not fatal, to the advocates and organizations who have dedicated their existence to repaying our Nation's debt to the citizens it was unable to protect.

I hope we will not abandon victims in their hour of greatest need. I hope we remember the reason we are all here today; above all, I hope we remember the crime victim.

○

80-935 - 95 (80)